HOLLYWOOD
on the Links

HOLLYWOOD
on the Links

A Collection of the Greatest
Celebrity Golf Stories of All Time

Tom Cunneff

With a Foreword by Jack Lemmon

CB
CONTEMPORARY BOOKS

Library of Congress Cataloging-in-Publication Data

Cunneff, Tom.
   Hollywood on the links : a collection of the greatest celebrity golf
stories of all time / Tom Cunneff ; foreword by Jack Lemmon.
      p.   cm.
   ISBN 0-8092-2945-5
   1. Golf—Anecdotes.   2. Celebrities—Anecdotes.   I. Title.
GV967.C88   1997
796.352—dc21   97-43787
                                                            CIP

All interior and back cover photos copyright © Tom Cunneff except the following:
Photo on p. 10 copyright © J. D. Cuban/Allsport. Photos on pp. 58, 76, and 121
copyright © Allan Grant. Photos on pp. 64 and 98 copyright © Craig Jones/Allsport.
Photo on p. 98 copyright © 1997 Art Streiber/Creative Photographers, Inc. Author
photo on back cover by Helen K. Garber

Cover design by Kim Bartko
Cover illustration copyright © Todd L. W. Doney
Interior design by Amy Ng

Published by Contemporary Books
A division of NTC/Contemporary Publishing Group, Inc.
4255 West Touhy Avenue, Lincolnwood (Chicago), Illinois 60646-1975 U.S.A.
Copyright © 1998 by Tom Cunneff
Printed in the United States of America
International Standard Book Number: 0-8092-2945-5
18   17   16   15   14   13   12   11   10   9   8   7   6   5   4   3   2   1

For Betsy and Katie

Contents

Foreword

*I*t seems like everybody in Hollywood plays golf these days, and that's probably true to a certain extent. In my thirty-five years playing the game, I can't ever remember it being more popular. I suppose that's because it's a terrific diversion and marvelous release from what we do: the pressures of show business and the actual work involved in directing, writing, or acting. It's totally different. Because the game takes such concentration, most of the time you are capable of forgetting whatever the problems are, and all you're worried about is putting a ball in a hole that's too small.

Golf is the purest form of sport. There's nothing else like it. The wonderful thing about it is, you're not playing against somebody else. I love the fact that above all there's no team—it's just you. You're out there really playing against yourself and your own weaknesses. As such, it can be the most frustrating game in the world, but it can also be the most rewarding. There's a tremendous satisfaction in being able to do something that's very difficult. We're all capable of hitting the shots, but can you do it when it counts? It's a matter of, can you do it now, *right now*? And then when you do pull it off, there's nobody around to see you hit that one-in-a-thousand shot.

I guess that's why so many wonderful stories come out of the game. You can't wait to tell your friends about the one that didn't get away, or the one that did. As you can see from this wonderful collection Tom has put together, there's always some crazy thing happening. It can be terribly funny, although at the moment it's not funny. Golf stories are also interesting because for anyone who plays the game they're easy to imagine. We've all been there.

Jack Lemmon
Los Angeles
October 1997

Preface

*H*ollywood celebrities aren't much different from the rest of us; they just get to play a lot more golf, be it at the ever-expanding schedule of charity tournaments or at their home course in Los Angeles. And it is at these storied clubs—Riviera, Lakeside, Hillcrest, and Bel-Air—that many of the events in this book take place. It's no coincidence that the clubs all sprang up in the 1920s when filmmaking in Hollywood really began to take off. They became the hangouts for such legends as Douglas Fairbanks, Humphrey Bogart, and Clark Gable. Now such current stars as Clint Eastwood, Jack Lemmon, and Kevin Costner roam their fairways.

If you want to see stars, don't bother buying a map to their homes or driving to Malibu Beach. Finagle an invite to Bel-Air and you just might see Jack Nicholson holding court at the large corner table in Bel-Air's grillroom while Sean Connery tees off on the par-3 10th just a few feet away. In this industry town, movie stars and golf are as closely linked as Beverly Hills and Rodeo Drive. To many, it means more to be known as a player on the links than a "player" in Hollywood.

One of the great things about golf is how wonderfully it lends itself to storytelling. Because the game continually tests the traits of character—patience, inner fortitude, grace under pressure, a sense of humor—it is a natural stage for high drama and comedy. Perhaps that's why so many actors are drawn to it. Some of their best performances occur with no camera or audience in sight.

That so many wonderful tales can emerge from one game is even more amazing when you consider that just about three minutes out of a typical four-hour round is actually spent hitting the ball! And what a game it is that those few minutes can produce hours of stories. With the help of the traditional postround libation, these memories are cemented in our minds forever. We can recall minute details of great shots (and bad) hit years ago, and like a good wine, they get better (or worse) with age. Toss in a celebrity and a crowd like those they get at the AT&T Pebble Beach National Pro-Am and the stories become forged to perfection. Indeed, celebrity golf has gotten so popular, they've even got their own televised tour now. Whom would you rather see bogey a hole, Michael Jordan or Omar Uresti?

You have to admire celebrities who are willing to put it on the line in tournaments, especially those that are televised. They're out there alone, naked, stripped of their celluloid heroics. Their carefully crafted images are at stake. That's why some don't play in them (Jack Nicholson and Sylvester Stallone come to mind). A press agent can't do a damn thing for them, and that's the beauty of it. You get to see them as real human beings. In an industry where billions are spent on make-believe, the one thing you can't fake is a good golf game.

Though a few of the stories in this book will be familiar to readers, most are original, never-before-told tales. Unfortunately, the distaff set is woefully underrepresented. Like action films, the game, by and large, is still a male bastion, belonging more to the stars than the starlets.

Acknowledgments

*W*hen I was thinking of a subject to tackle for my first book, someone suggested I write about a topic I like because I'd be spending a lot of time on it. It was great advice. The only thing I enjoy more than writing about golf is playing it. Except for some tedious hours transcribing interview tapes, this book has never felt like work.

The idea for the book sprang from a piece I wrote on celebrity golfers for the program of the 1995 PGA Championship at Riviera Country Club. I'd like to thank the editor of that story, Dwayne Netland, for introducing me to a subject with so much color and history.

Many thanks, as well, to my agent, Scott Waxman, for his input and commercial savvy; my editor at Contemporary Books, Matthew Carnicelli, for his guidance, belief, and insight; project editor Craig Bolt, for making me look good; the managing editor of *People* magazine, Carol Wallace, and West Coast Bureau Chief Jack Kelley, for their permission and understanding; and my wonderful wife, Betsy, who has allowed me to pursue my obsession with golf at the expense of many a weekend morning. Most of all, I'd like to thank the celebrities who gave of their time, especially Jack Lemmon. Without them, there'd be no *Hollywood on the Links*.

There are many other people who contributed to the book in some way, or just helped me become a better golfer or better golf writer. They are: Michael Arkush, David Barrett, Richard Bermudez and the Boys of Rancho San Joaquin, Warren Cowan, Joe Cunneff, Shirley Cunneff, Cynthia Dadonna, Ron Del Barrio, Clint Dimond, Raymond Floyd, Jim Frank, Eddie Gannon, Todd Gold, Danford Greene, John Griffiths, Chris Hodenfield, John Marin, Peter McCleery, Gary McCord, Jim Murray, Randy Peterson, Todd Phillips, Jeff Sanderson, Ron "Ballwash" Shelton, Scott Simpson, Sam Snead, and Craig Tomashoff. Thank you all.

Finally, I'd like to thank my late father, Dr. Raymond Cunneff, for teaching me this great game and sharing his love of it. Nobody enjoyed a good golf story more.

HOLLYWOOD
on the *Links*

Fred Astaire

One of Hollywood's most stylish stars ever, Fred Astaire had an incredibly smooth swing, not surprisingly. He played to about a 10-handicap at Bel-Air Country Club, where actor Robert Wagner first met the dancer in the 1940s when he was a caddie at the club. "I loved playing with Fred," says Wagner, who usually would play nine holes with Astaire early in the morning after joining the club himself. "He loved the game, but like all actors, you play for a while then you have to let it go, because you've got to go to work. He was a perfectionist who would play a lot, but then he would have to start rehearsing."

One day at Bel-Air, Astaire did a few impromptu dance steps before teeing off and decided to use the routine in his upcoming 1938 movie, *Carefree*, his most comic outing with Ginger Rogers. In the film, Astaire hits a row of golf balls while tap-dancing. To perfect the sequence, Fred had to rehearse for ten days. Five men had to shag three hundred golf balls. A piano was needed so Astaire could keep his rhythm as were several cases of beer to combat the ninety-five-degree heat at the RKO ranch, an outdoor studio in the desert. The scene took two and a half days to film. The result: three minutes of on-screen action.

Shari Belafonte

*H*arry's middle daughter—best known for the TV series *Hotel* and those ads for Weight Watchers—is a 50-handicap (she once was an 80!). But then, she plays only once a month. "I play in a lot of these celebrity golf tournaments. My handicap is so bad I'm actually great for the team," admits the actress, who's been playing for about ten years. "I've got a good short game. And as a complete fluke, every once in a while I hit a drive that's unbelievable."

Indeed, Shari won the long-drive contest with a poke of 230 yards at a recent celebrity tournament in Puerto Rico at the El Conquistador. With her was her actor-husband, Sam Behrens of *Sunset Beach*, and her younger brother David, who killed one of the ubiquitous iguanas on the course with one of his drives.

"We didn't actually see it happen," Shari says. "It's just that his ball was a foot and a half away from this just-dead iguana. I'll never let him forget it. I call him 'iguana killer' now."

*S*hari's husband, Sam, is the real fanatic in the family. He's such a diehard that he wanted to replace the pool in their Los Angeles home with a sand trap and forgo expanding the master bedroom to make room for a putting green. Belafonte nixed the bunker idea rather quickly. "We did have a serious discussion about installing the putting green," she says. "But then I reminded him what we did in the master bedroom."

*B*elafonte's best score is a 114. She was on pace to shatter that mark a few years ago at Doral in Miami while playing with Sam—in a torrential downpour, no less. She broke 50 on the front and was having the round of her life.

"I had just bought a brand-new outfit," she recalls. "It was red madras. The red was just dripping down my body. I looked like fresh kill. I was wearing those real bulky V. G. Smith socks. They were literally dragging in the mud like little trains on a wedding dress." Much to Shari's chagrin, they had to quit after eleven holes since the rain had gotten so heavy they could no longer see the ball after hitting it.

Humphrey Bogart

Though he was nicknamed "Bogey," Humphrey Bogart was much better than a bogey golfer. He was a single-digit handicapper and belonged to Lakeside Golf Club, not far from Warner Brothers studios, where he made many of his gangster pictures. He used to ride his bike over to the club. One of his biggest fans was a caddie at the club, Staggering Haggerty. "Whenever Bogey would come up, Haggerty would make believe he was holding a machine gun and give him that rat-a-tat-tat," says Eddie Gannon, who's worked at Lakeside since 1936. "One day, Haggerty started to do it and Bogey pulled out a prop machine gun with blanks in it from Warner Brothers. He said, 'Haggerty, I've had enough of you,' and started shooting at him. Haggerty ran like hell."

Apparently Bogart wasn't the most beloved person at the club. Legend has it that W. C. Fields, who was a regular fixture at Lakeside because of his love of golf and the fact that he lived on the other side of the lake, was about to tee off on number 1 when the starter sent Bogart out to join him. Fields took one look at Bogart and said, "If I wanted to play with a dick, I'd play with my own."

*I*n his 1985 golf memoir, *Confessions of a Hooker,* Bob Hope recalled that Bogey was "a low-handicap golfer, although for some reason not many people remember that. The last time I saw Bogey it was in my hotel room in England. He and Lauren Bacall were returning home from doing USO shows in Italy. We started drinking, and pretty soon Bogey suggested I lie down on the floor. He wanted to tee up a ball on a piece of gum on my nose and take a swat at it with my driver. And I let him do it. I haven't been able to breathe properly since that time. But it was fun."

*L*os Angeles Times columnist Jim Murray was having dinner in the late fifties with Bogart at the legendary Romanoff's in Beverly Hills when the subject of golf came up. "What the hell do you know about golf?" Bogart asked. "As Mike Romanoff used to say, 'After two drinks Bogart turned into Bogart,'" says Murray, whose response to Bogey was, "Hell, I know as much about golf as you do." Said Bogart: "Oh, so you think so? Can you come down to Tamarisk on Thursday?" At that very difficult course in the California desert, Bogey shot an 82. "He used 2-irons, difficult clubs," Murray recalls. "I was flabbergasted, but then I realized Bogart always wanted people to think he was a dead-end kid who came from Hell's Kitchen.

Lot of bullshit. His father was a Park Avenue Society doctor. He went to either Phillips Exeter or Andover. He knew how to sail, he knew how to play tennis and golf."

Bogey enjoyed watching the pros when they came to town, too. Before there were gallery ropes, he used to sit under the tree to the left of the 12th green at Riviera, sipping from time to time from a thermos full of bourbon.

George Clooney

Clooney and his best friends love to take golfing vacations together, piling into his Winnebago for weeks at a time with Clooney picking up most, if not all, of the tab. There have been seven or so of these trips. In 1993, they started at Pebble Beach, playing all the courses on the Monterey Peninsula, then continued on to Washington, Idaho, and Canada. The trip lasted three weeks.

George doesn't always have to pick up the tab, though. In May 1995, Planet Hollywood paid for the actor and four friends to take a four-city golf tour: Miami, Orlando, New Orleans, and Las Vegas. All he had to do was stop by the Planet Hollywood in each city and sign a few autographs.

During the week between Christmas and New Year's 1995, Clooney took six of his buddies to the Big Island of Hawaii, where he paid the $300-a-night hotel suites at the Mauna Lani and Mauna Kea resorts along with the $100-a-round greens' fees on the hotels' courses. "That's part of who he is," says one friend who was there, actor Matt Adler. "He will do what he can for his friends. He wanted to go to Hawaii and play golf with his friends. Some could afford it, some couldn't."

As for Clooney's game, Adler adds, "He's not a guy you want to gamble against. When you're sure that he's out of the hole, he's the guy who will come back with an evil laugh and sink a sixty-foot putt to take it away from you. He's got that confidence about him."

"His luck is the best in the world," says another friend and actor who was with Clooney in Hawaii, Richard Kind of ABC's *Spin City*. "In Hawaii, there's lava on either side of the fairway. He would hit into the lava and it would bounce back into the fairway 120 yards farther than any of us. He'd hit a tree and his ball would bounce onto the green. It was unbelievable."

After one of the rounds, the gang was lounging by the pool when a woman sent over a note to Clooney offering "sex, no strings attached." George took a pass. He was there to golf.

Sean Connery

*A*s a Scotsman, Sean Connery is almost required by law to play golf. He grew up in Edinburgh, where the game is simply a way of life, but he was much more interested in becoming a professional soccer player—or footballer—than a golfer. It wasn't until his acting career was well under way that he started to play regularly. According to Michael Freedland's 1994 biography of the star, Connery got hooked on golf in the late 1950s after an actor-friend, Daniel Massey, took up the game.

"I claim responsibility for turning Sean into a golf bore," Massey's wife, actress Andrienne Corri, told Freedland. "As any woman married to an actor will tell you, the biggest problem is that they are always in the house, always under your feet. . . . Well, I hit on the idea of suggesting that Dan should take up golf. I didn't realize how serious he would become about it."

One day Massey was just about to leave his house to go play a round when Connery dropped by. What followed was nearly epoch-making in view of what has happened since. "Ah, golf," said Sean, "I think I've got some clubs somewhere."

"Soon they were both secretly taking lessons from the same pro and there was a deadly rivalry between them," said Corri. Freedland notes that it was only because Connery's nascent acting career was going so well that he felt free enough to devote a lot of time to the game.

Sean Connery, Lexus Challenge, La Quinta, California, 1996

Connery's dedication to the game really began in earnest, however, with his third outing as James Bond in 1964's *Goldfinger*, in which Bond outsmarts the titular villain, played by German actor Gert Frobe, to whom winning is everything. Their match for a shilling a hole turns into one for £5,000 during the final two holes.

When Frobe putts out on 17, Connery retrieves the ball from the hole and pulls a switch, tossing him a Slazenger 7, not the Slazenger 1 he had been playing with. Frobe thinks he wins the match 1-up on the 18th when a quickly playing Connery misses a five-footer to tie with Frobe's ball still in the cup (there's no penalty for this, by the way, according to the USGA).

"Weren't you playing a Slazenger 1?" asks a smirking Connery, studying the balls after picking them up out of the cup. "You must have played the wrong ball somewhere on the 18th fairway. I'm afraid you lose the hole and the match."

Connery, if it is indeed he, is shown hitting only one full shot, a drive on the 17th, but it looks suspiciously like he has a double agent filling in for him, since the swing looks like that of a pro, or at least a very-low-handicap player, and the person's face is obscured. It's probably not Connery, since a high-handicap Bond wouldn't have done at all. It was important that he look as competent on the golf course as he does at a baccarat table.

To prepare for the scene, Connery took lessons from the pros at Stoke Poges Golf Club, near London, which doubled as the fictitious Royal St. Marks links in the movie. By the end, Freedland notes, Connery picked up golf the way other people pick up viruses, and it became an obsession he was never to lose. From that film on, he played for money every time he teed it up, sometimes £100 a hole, sometimes more.

Connery's poor upbringing still stayed with him in other ways, however. For £12 a year, he became a member of the Stage Golfing Society. For £1 a month, he could play at some of the finest courses in the land—even Wentworth, Freedland reports. The only problem was that there were no privileges on weekends.

While having lunch during the making of *Goldfinger* with Bond producer Cubby Broccoli and others, Ted Moore, the director of photography, asked Connery if he was playing that weekend. "No," he replied. "Well," Moore responded, "how about a game on Saturday?" Connery shook his head. "No," he said. "I only really like playing at Wentworth and I can't play on Saturdays." An incredulous Moore suggested paying a greens fee, but Connery didn't take too kindly to the recommendation, according to Freedland. Unnecessary expenditure was not on his agenda then.

He doesn't mind paying greens fees these days, though. Now about a 12-handicap, Connery belongs to four clubs, including St. Andrews, Pine Valley, and Bel-Air. Twice he's won the Silver Jubilee Tournament at St. Andrews, in which the entire conclave of members from all over the world comes into town each September to participate. He insisted during a BBC interview that "winning the Silver Jubilee gave me more pleasure than winning my Oscar" for *The Untouchables* the same year, 1987.

*I*n December 1996, Connery teamed with pro Hale Irwin to win the Lexus Challenge in La Quinta, California, beating out Kevin Costner, who was paired with Lee Trevino, and ten other teams. In the two-day event, they shot a record-setting 21-under-par score, shattering the 17-under mark set by host Raymond Floyd and actor Michael Chiklis in the inaugural event the previous year. Connery recorded thirteen net birdies over the two days, to Irwin's nine natural birdies. They bogeyed only once in the two rounds.

The second day, Connery shot 3 over par on the front nine, but, then, he came to the tournament well prepared, having played fourteen straight days at St. Andrews in the autumn meeting. He's played in the event every year since he became a member of St. Andrews more than twenty years ago. He carries his own bag, too.

"There are no buggies [golf carts] allowed on the course except for medical reasons," the actor said after his victory. "The course is relatively flat, but it's the wind and rain that give you the most difficulty, along with some pretty tough bunkers."

*W*hen Connery received the news that James Bond creator Ian Fleming had died in 1964, he and fellow actor Rex Harrison paid the author a tribute by playing eighteen holes at Rome's Olgiata Course, hitting the Penfold Hearts balls Bond used in the golf course scene in *Goldfinger*.

Mike Connors

*T*he star of the 1967–75 television series *Mannix*, Mike Connors plays to an 18-handicap, but there was one brief, shining moment a few years ago at his home club, Bel-Air, where his play resembled that of a pro. One of the club's best golfers, Jim Garner, was about to tee off with two other low handicappers, when they saw Connors. "Hey, Mike, we need a fourth," Garner called out to him. "Ahh, you guys are too good," Connors responded. "What's the difference?" one of the others said. "C'mon out."

Connors agreed to play the front nine with them and proceeded to par the first and second holes before birdieing the third, a downhill par 3. He bogeyed the fourth but stood on the par 3 5th tee even par, much to his astonishment. Then the unthinkable happened. Using a 5-iron from about 150 yards, he aced the hole. "It hit right on the front of the green and it rolled all the way back to the pin and went in," Connors recalls. "The funny part is I didn't see it go in because the pin was kind of in the shadows. The caddie was standing up there, and he yelled, 'Hole-in-one!' And we said, 'Who?' He said, 'You!' I was in complete shock."

Counting his stroke, Connors ended up with a zero on the hole. After five holes, he was 2 under par gross, 7 under with his full handicap. His partners thought they were getting hustled. "They said, 'Hey, what is this? Are you giving us a con job?' I said, 'Believe me,

I'm playing so far over my head.' They said, 'Well, now you've got to play the whole eighteen holes and buy everybody a drink.'"

Connors played the best nine holes of his life, shooting a 38. He showed he wasn't a hustler by ballooning on the back side with a 46. "But the first five holes were incredible," he says. "I've never played that well in my life. It was just one of those days. The fun part was doing it with three sensational golfers."

A converted tennis player, Connors started playing golf in the early 1980s when he was performing in a play in Florida and was staying on a golf course with his wife, Mary Lou. His second attempt at taking up the game worked out a lot better than his first back in the early fifties at the urging of his wife, who had just started:

"I was talked into playing in Chuck Connors's tournament in Palm Springs at the Canyon Club," he recalls. "I got on the first tee and I sliced my first ball into the parking lot out-of-bounds. The second ball I hit struck the palm trees on the right and fell onto the ladies' tee. With the crowd there, I was so goddamn embarrassed I couldn't see straight. My wife, who was watching, said, 'I can't stand this,' and she left. About an hour later, she got in a cart with a friend to see how I was doing. They stopped at a tee and the guy said, 'Would you look at the friggin' idiot on the wrong fairway going the wrong way.' When she saw it was me, she said, 'Let's get out of here. I don't even want to see this anymore.' After that I gave up the game completely." He was so traumatized by the whole experience that it was a good thirty years until he picked up a club again.

Alice Cooper

You know golf has crossed over from its starchy, country-club roots when you discover that the original dark prince of rock, Alice Cooper, plays the game. He's a self-described "golf rat" who bases his tours on where the best golf courses are, the better to keep his 4-handicap in tune. When he's not on the road he's at home in Scottsdale, Arizona, where he tees it up often with tour pros Tom Lehman and Steve Jones. He plays as much as five times a week at one of his two clubs, Moon Valley and the Arizona Biltmore.

But it was at another local club, Camelback, where four years ago he shot his career-best round, a 67, the framed scorecard for which hangs on his wall at home. "The nice thing was I was playing with some local pros, so I won seventeen skins," he recalls. "I didn't even collect the money. I said, 'Guys, just sign the card.' I wasn't even counting my score. I got to the par-5 18th and I said, 'What do I got going here?' They said, 'If you par this hole you'll shoot 69.' I hit a 3-wood over the green and chipped it in for an eagle and a 67. These guys just threw their clubs up and said, 'That's it.' The next day I went out and shot 78 or 79, but at least I had that day. I was possessed." And if anybody knows about being possessed, it's Cooper.

*C*ooper, who harbors a dream of playing the Senior Tour ("I'd put a little color into it," he says), has had two holes-in-one and two double eagles. More amazingly, his ten-year-old son, Dash, who's been playing only for a year, just had a hole in one at the 6th hole at Cabo del Sol in Cabo San Lucas, the rocker's favorite course. "He knocked it in from 154 yards with my driver," he explains, still flabbergasted over the feat. "I keep telling him, 'Ben Hogan never had one, and you're ten years old and you've had one already!'"

A recovering alcoholic, Cooper took up the game fifteen years ago when he quit drinking (he used to down two bottles of whiskey a day). After undergoing treatment and getting out of the hospital, he played eighteen to thirty-six holes a day every day for a year. Now, he "only" gets out five or six times a week. "As bad habits go, an even tradeoff," he says. "I'm an extremist. When I quit drinking and started golfing, I became an extremist golfer."

But, please, if you should see Cooper leave a putt short in one of the many pro-ams he plays in, don't shout out to him, "Nice, putt, Alice. Does your husband play, too?" "I can't tell you how many times I hear that," he says, shaking his head. "All the time."

Kevin Costner, Lexus Challenge, La Quinta, California, 1997

Kevin Costner

*B*efore he made the film *Tin Cup*, Kevin Costner rarely played golf—maybe once a year with his former father-in-law while on vacation. "I could never justify four or five hours a day working at the game," he told John Feinstein in *Premiere* magazine. But playing the part of Roy "Tin Cup" McAvoy, a washed-up West Texas range pro who almost wins the U.S. Open, gave him all the justification he needed. Costner picked up his play in Hawaii while shooting *Waterworld*, but when he first started working with *Tin Cup*'s technical consultant, journeyman touring pro, and CBS commentator Gary McCord, in August 1995, just a few weeks before filming was to begin, McCord took one look at Costner and told director Ron Shelton that they were going to have to find a stand-in. He didn't give up on the actor, however.

"I just said, 'We're going to try and make you look good, because we don't have enough time to do anything else,'" McCord recalls. "He had a big old loopy swing with a big full finish. We had to build a swing that was from West Texas. It had to be fast and have a real sudden, short finish," to keep the shot low in the legendary winds of the Lone Star State. "This guy can't have a follow-through."

But the athletic Costner quickly learned the swing; McCord had never seen anything like it. Still, Costner had his difficulties trying to recite his lines *and* play golf when shooting began in October at La Paloma Country Club in Tucson. "I don't know how he got all the script out and then tried to go, 'Okay, left toe flared out, knees bent, strong left-hand grip, take it back hands first,'" McCord says. "So he hit some goofy shots. He'd hit one really good one, then hit four in the condos."

The pressure became even more intense by the time the production made it to Houston's Kingwood Country Club the following month, where many real PGA Tour pros, like Corey Pavin and Fred Couples, had cameos. "This was tantamount to taking your child to graduation," McCord says. "He was pretty nervous, especially the last few days when we had eight thousand extras out there. I got nervous, too, because it was so narrow and Don [Johnson, the film's antagonist] and Kevin both had to hit shots. I'm back in our little tower with Ron and I said, 'Someone's going to die here today. There's going to be an ugly Titleist death here.' But it went okay. A few people got hit, but they were glancing blows."

*O*ne day during filming of a U.S. Open scene in front of thousands of extras, Costner had to sink a fifteen-foot putt. Eleven, twelve takes later, he was still trying to make it. Director Shelton motioned McCord over and said, "Go tell him something."

"Costner was walking around mystified," McCord recalls. "I thought we were going to be out there forever. So I walked up to him and said, 'I'm getting hungry. Why don't you sink this son of a bitch so we can get out of here?'" It worked. Costner sank the putt and the "gallery" finally got to cheer.

A barren cow pasture outside Sonoita, Arizona, not far from the Mexican border, served as the site on which the crew constructed McAvoy's driving range. So convincing—and appealing—an oasis was it that passersby attempted to pull in to swat a bucket of balls. But only the cast and crew got to use it.

"There was a telephone pole at the end of the driving range," Shelton says. "We had forty zillion range balls, so in between camera setups, Kevin and the guys would just hit these shots out into the night. One night Kevin bet someone that he could hit the telephone pole, which was out about 240 yards. He hit it not only on the first try—he hit it three out of ten tries. I could stand there for fifty years and not hit it. There's absolutely no exaggeration in this. Everybody was stunned. Tiger Woods couldn't do that."

That wasn't the only gambling that happened on the set. "We bet on everything the whole movie," the director adds. "We tried to hit everything with golf balls, telephone poles, rabbits, you name it. The downtime was very much like the movie. You couldn't quite tell when the camera was rolling. Guys would bet $100 on a four-foot putt. I remember Kevin lost one of those and I said, 'Kevin, bet 'em a million dollars,' and nobody would take the bet because for a million dollars the other guy would get nervous."

A fter filming on the movie wrapped, Costner, playing to about a 16-handicap, went on tour and teed it up in the Bob Hope, Phoenix, and AT&T tournaments. "He went out and showed his golf game to the world in only two or three months of really understanding what the game was about," says McCord, who played with the actor in the Hope and was jittery over the prospect. "Here he is playing in a professional golf tournament and he knows nothing about golf. Before he teed off, I was thinking, 'Don't hit that lady right there on the forehead.' He hit the prettiest 225-yard 2-iron, right down the middle. My heart was pounding. He just picked up the tee and winked."

But even Costner would admit he looked better than he actually played. Preparing to tee off as a gallery crowded around him at Pebble Beach, he said, "It's scary to think these people assume I know what I'm doing."

*N*ot long after the movie was released, Costner and the organizers of the Hassan II Golf Trophy, a ten-day extravaganza in Morocco hosted by King Hassan II, had reached an agreement to bring the star in as an amateur participant until Costner's agent demanded a $400,000-a-day appearance fee. Tournament officials blanched at the $4 million price tag and rescinded the invite. Maybe he just needed a little incentive. As he told John Feinstein on the set, "Yes, I find myself liking golf more now, but I still think finding five hours a day for it when this movie is over is going to be tough for me."

Richard Crenna

Richard Crenna, who has had leading roles in such films as *Body Heat*, the *Rambo* series, and numerous TV movies, started playing while attending USC in the 1940s. He took his first lessons from legendary pro Lighthorse Harry Cooper at Lakeside Golf Club. "He would only let me practice with a 5-iron," recalls the actor, who now plays to a 17-handicap (he was once an 8). "He wouldn't let me on the course for many, many lessons. When I went on the course, he insisted I only take my 5-iron."

Like many celebrities, some of Crenna's fondest memories come from his years playing Bing Crosby's Clambake at Pebble Beach. He was playing with Bel-Air's pro, Eddie Merrins, in 1968 when the wind was howling off the Pacific right into their faces as they came to the short, downhill, par-3 7th. "It's ordinarily a little pitching wedge," Crenna recalls. "I was a fairly good hitter then and I just barely got a 2-wood to the green. Eddie hit a 2-iron and knocked it in the hole. He aced it! In those days, he didn't even get a cup. Everybody just said, 'Nice shot, Ed.' Now he'd be driving around in a convertible."

It was also about that time that Crenna helped his good friend, Tony Lema, win the tournament. It was unusually cold and Lema was having trouble keeping warm. Crenna happened to have a big down hunting coat in his car back at the Lodge, since he had driven down from up north to play in the event. At the 8th hole, he asked a martial if he could borrow a cart.

"The wind was absolutely freezing," he says. "I raced back to my car, came back, and caught him about a hole later and gave him the coat, which he wore between every shot. At the end of the round, he autographed the coat, writing, 'I never could have done it without you.' I still have it."

*C*renna's most vivid golf memory is of a pilgrimage he made to St. Andrews in 1956, when he played the Old Course for the first time. He can still recall almost every shot. "I didn't even have my own clubs," says Crenna, who had to borrow a beat-up set with hickory shafts, and was paired with some local Scotsmen. "I walked over to pay and the man said, 'That's all taken care of. Your partners want you to be their guest today, since it's your first time at St. Andrews.' So I played with these two old codgers. I had a caddie who looked like Barry Fitzgerald. He had a little tiny stub pipe with a piece of tape around the middle of it. He had a tie and jacket on. He looked like he was going to church, not going to caddie."

Crenna opened with a beautiful drive that left him a 7-iron, or so he thought, to the green. His caddie shook his head and said, "Hitchure fave." Crenna stubbornly said, "No, no, I can reach that easily with a 7." "Of course, I was twenty yards short," he says with a laugh. "That went on for the first four holes. I never listened to his advice. Finally I just said to him, 'I'll hit the ball, you just put the club in my hand and tell me where to aim.' I ended up shooting an 82. It was one of the most memorable rounds of my entire life, because I can remember that day so clearly."

One of Crenna's first major films was 1952's *The Pride of St. Louis*, the story of big-league pitchers Daffy and Dizzy Dean. Crenna played Daffy and Dan Dailey played Dizzy. "Dan was not really a ballplayer," Crenna says. "Dan could barely get the ball to the plate. I had been an athlete my whole life. I could throw the ball pretty well. We had a guy, Ike Danning, who had been a minor-league catcher and was hired to work out with us. I'd get out and just wing it in. We'd look at each other like, 'What do we do now?'"

They were shooting the picture at 20th Century-Fox, where the Ben Hogan story, *Follow the Sun*, had been completed the year before. Much of that movie was shot in a big open field bordered by trees next to the studio. (The area is now a huge office and shopping complex called Century City.) "So Ike said, 'You play golf, right? You'll throw your arm out if we work out all day. Let's hit some balls,' so we used to go out there on the *Follow the Sun* fairway and practice our golf."

Bing Crosby

*A*long with Jack Lemmon, Bing Crosby is the Hollywood personality most identified with the game. His "Clambake," which he first held in 1937 at Rancho Santa Fe Country Club, near San Diego, began the special bond that exists between celebrities and professional golfers.

At his best, Bing was a 2-handicap who won the Lakeside club championship four times (1936, '37, '42, and '43). He also played in both the U.S. and British Amateur Championships. Every time Bing would break 70 he'd buy his caddie, Leonard "Snake" Arnold, a new suit. "I don't think Bing had too many bad lies," recalls Sam Snead, who won the first two Clambakes and played in many subsequent ones. One day, after Bing shot 69 at Bel-Air Country Club, Snake turned to him as they were heading to the clubhouse and said, "If it's just the same to you, I think I'll take the money this time, because my tailor is on holiday." Crosby laughed and happily obliged.

A terrific tale, which Crosby recounted to Norman Blackburn in Lakeside Golf Club's fiftieth-anniversary book, was right out of *Tin Cup*. Bing Crosby did not like to lose. One day at the club in

1940, after he lost a match to a top-notch golfer and hustler by the name of John Montague, they were sitting in the bar. "You didn't give me enough strokes," Crosby complained, to which Montague responded, "I could beat you with a shovel, a bat, and a rake." The bet: $5 a hole, which was a lot in those days.

Montague was a big, strong guy and knocked his "drive" with the bat into a greenside bunker on the first hole, a short par 4. Crosby hit a 6-iron for his second shot about thirty feet from the hole. "I thought we might halve it," Bing recalled. But Montague "shoveled" his ball two feet from the cup after scooping it up, sand and all. "Naturally, I was a bit shaken up and I putted about three feet past the pin. John walks up and says, 'That's good, pal,' and knocked my ball away. He then took the rake, used it like a pool cue, and knocked it right into the cup [for a birdie]. I was 'history.' "

*U*sually if Crosby lost, he'd talk his opponent into playing for double or nothing over holes 1, 2, and 3 or "the whiskey route" (so called because it came after a few drinks). One time a guy by the name of "Shaggy" Wolf beat him out of a couple hundred bucks, and Bing was not in the least bit pleased, since his normal game was a $5 nassau.

"Shaggy had him beat all ways, so they played the whiskey route," recalls Lakeside's starter, Eddie Gannon, who's worked at the club since the 1930s. "Shaggy, who was ahead of Bing about twenty, thirty yards to the right, knocked his ball on the green and Bing called him on it for playing out of turn. He made him play the shot over, and Shaggy dumped it in the trap. Bing beat him and won all his money back. The next day, Shaggy took him to small-claims court for the $200. It made the front page of the paper."

The two settled their differences out of court and Wolf dropped the suit.

Crosby's son Nathaniel started playing golf with his dad at their home course, Burlingame Country Club, outside San Francisco, when he was seven. Nathaniel became quite a good player rather quickly, beating his dad for the first time at age eleven. Bing loved to watch his son compete in junior tournaments, even though he didn't always have the best view.

"Whenever he would watch me in a match, he'd bring a gallery with him because people would congregate around him," recalls Nathaniel, now president of the Nicklaus Golf Equipment Company. "Whenever he'd be watching me in a tournament, there'd be, like, fifty or sixty people trying to rub elbows with him. So a lot of times what my dad would do is watch me from two holes over with a pair of binoculars. I see a group of people a couple of holes over and I'd say, 'Yup, my dad must be over there.'"

Almost four years after Bing's passing, Nathaniel won the U.S. Amateur in 1981 in a dramatic 1-up victory over Brian Lindley at the Olympic Club in San Francisco. Bing no doubt would have been extremely proud to have seen him accomplish such a feat. Nathaniel believes he did witness it. "My line back then was that he had a better view of it than the Goodyear blimp," Nathaniel says. "If we have a little faith, we can assume that was the case."

Mac Davis

*M*ac Davis is so addicted to golf that he's taken to writing songs about the game. He retooled one of his hits, "Hard to Be Humble," with golf lyrics and sings it in a commercial for Callaway golf clubs.

Maybe if the singer devoted as much time to his career as he has to his golf game he'd still be the movie and musical force he was in the 1970s. Davis, a 4-handicap and Bel-Air Country Club member, has been playing twenty-five years and still retains a piece of advice he received when he first started from a composer-friend, Gordon Jenkins. "He shot in the 80s with one of those adjustable clubs that you can turn into any loft you want," Davis explains. "And he was in his 70s at the time. I just asked him, 'Gosh, what's your secret?' He said, 'Mac, golf is a waltz. You're a musician. It's "rock-a-bye, baby." You rock onto your right side and you spank the baby. It's the rhythm of it, it's one-two-three, hit.' I've never forgotten that. Every time I get in trouble with my swing, that's what I go to. It slows me down, and it's a nice memory to have, too."

*D*avis is a bit of a scrambler on the course. "I'm not consistent off the tee," he says. "I tell everybody I have to regrip my lob wedge and my ball fetcher about once a week." His ability to get up and down never came in more handy than during a quarterfinal match about seven years ago in the Bel-Air club championship against sixteen-time champion Ted Richards. Shooting a 73, Davis took only twenty-one putts to beat Richards 1-up when he sunk a twenty-five-footer on the last hole. But when you live by the lob wedge, you die by it, and in the next round he lost to Jack Wagner of *Melrose Place*.

*T*he funniest moment Davis ever had on a course came soon after he began playing, when he had just started performing in Las Vegas. He and another Vegas entertainer, Buddy Greco, were playing at the Tropicana course and Greco hit one of his tee shots out of bounds. "He angrily stomped up, hit another shot, which he put in the fairway bunker," Davis recalls. "He was really angry, because he had a good round going up until then. From out of the bunker, he hit a career shot, an 8-iron about four inches from the cup for a gimme bogey. He turned around and looked at me like, 'That'll teach you.' He stomped out of the trap and stepped right on a trap rake. It flew up and hit him square in the nose, almost knocked him out. It actually vibrated, like in the cartoons. I was rolling on the grass, and he was standing there trying to throttle the rake. He had his hands around it trying to choke it. That's the biggest laugh I've ever had."

John Denver

t's fitting that the last thing John Denver did before his death in a plane crash in October 1997 was play golf. He loved the game. The bespectacled "country boy" was an accomplished 11-handicap who belonged to the Maroon Creek Club in Aspen, Colorado. He often played in Monterey, California, where he also owned a home. On that fateful day, Denver played a round with friends at Spyglass Hill Golf Course before driving to Monterey Peninsula Airport.

It was Denver's father, Henry John ("Dutch") Deutschendorf Sr., a hard-drinking Air Force test pilot, who taught his son how to fly. Dutch was also a scratch golfer who introduced John to the game. John used to caddie for him as a kid, but he didn't seriously start playing the game himself until ten years ago. "Since that time I've really gotten hooked," said the singer just a few months before his death. "I think it's the greatest game in the world. You go out and you find circumstances where an architect has enhanced the natural habitat. You hit a ball, and as you begin to watch it take off you lose sight of the ball looking at the view."

Eighteen years ago his dad was giving him a hard time about something when John tried to put a stop to it. "I said, 'Excuse me, sir. I'm thirty-five years old. I've got a wife and a family. I've got my own home. I'm a hardworking man. I'm a very successful man. In fact, I'm a star, and I don't think I have to take that from you anymore.' And my dad, who was a big man, kind of shrugged his shoulders and chuckled a little bit. He said, 'Okay, I'll buy most of that. But I'll tell you when you're a star. When you get invited to Pebble Beach to play in that golf tournament, you'll be a star in my book.' "

Denver finally made it to the AT&T Pebble Beach National Pro-Am six years ago. Unfortunately, Dutch wasn't around to see him become "a star." He died in 1982.

*W*hen the composer of "Annie's Song" and "Rocky Mountain High" played the AT&T his second year, he was one of seven celebrities invited to play the star shoot-out, which is held over holes 1, 2, 3, 17, and 18. "I'm not quite comfortable with the situation," he said. "I'm very much in awe of not only the place, the tradition of the course, but the people that I'm with."

Jack Lemmon and Clint Eastwood bowed out on the first hole, Joe Pesci on the second, and Craig T. Nelson on the third. On the 17th, Glen Campbell fell out, leaving Denver against Bill Murray on the famed par-5 18th. "I'm looking down the fairway," Denver continued. "We've got the Pacific Ocean on the left, thousands of people on the right. A television camera right beside us. It could have been the U.S. Open."

After hitting a decent tee shot, Denver was strutting down the fairway in a "zone." Both he and Murray reached the green in four. When Murray just missed his twenty-footer for par, Denver was left with a straight-in, fifteen-foot putt for the win. "I addressed the ball, and with thousands of people around it gets quiet the way it can only get quiet on a golf course," he recounted. "Just as I'm about to stroke the ball, Bill says, 'Wait a minute!' at the top of his voice. He gets the whole crowd on their feet, cheering me to make this putt. This goes on for about ten minutes."

Denver, of course, had to back off the putt. "I got up to address the ball again and a seagull overhead starts laughing at me. I had to step away again. The crowd chuckles. It takes a couple minutes to quiet down. Phil Harris is over on the side, saying, 'This kid hasn't got a chance to keep it on the green.' I step up a third time, and just as I'm about to hit the ball Bill says, 'Put it in the cup, John,' right in the middle of my backswing. I closed my eyes and hit the ball. It hit the back of the cup, bounced about a foot in the air, and went in. It was a great moment, and one I'll never forget."

William Devane

William Devane never does anything easy. He always goes full tilt, whether it's his acting career, his business ventures, or his golf swing. The *Knots Landing* star takes a huge cut at the ball, resulting in a pronounced left-to-right ball flight. The shape of his shot caused him a little bit of concern coming into the final hole of the 1997 Lexus Challenge in La Quinta, California. He and his pro partner, Raymond Floyd, were four back of leaders Kevin Costner and Jim Colbert when they started the final round and five back when they made the turn. Then the pair went on an ornithological expedition, going seven under on their last five holes at the Citrus Course.

Floyd birdied 11, 12, 14, and 16, while Devane, playing to a 10-handicap, nabbed net eagles on the two par 5s, 15 and 17. "I think we've got a chance, pards," Floyd said to Devane as the actor prepared to tee off on the tough 395-yard par-4 18th, the number-two handicap hole. Devane needed to hit a good drive with his trusty 3-wood (he doesn't use a driver) to carry a set of traps on the left, and that's just what he did, leaving him 137 yards to the pin. But with the pin cut close to a water hazard on the left and bunkers back right, Devane was faced with a difficult shot. He wanted to hit it directly at the hole, but Floyd told him to aim well right, at the NBC sign. They settled on the Lexus sign, which was in between the two.

"I hit the shot and he said, 'You hit it right at the L, it's going right at the L!'" recalls Devane, who jumped on a 9-iron, which he usually hits about 130 yards. "I hit it right in there, pin high, about twenty feet right of the hole. If I really get after it, the ball goes straight. I knew I had to play right, but I didn't have any room for any ball movement."

A two-putt resulted in a par net birdie and a one-stroke victory. They made their incredible run, moreover, with the world's best golfer, Tiger Woods, following them. He's friends with Floyd's son, Robert, who was there to cheer his father on. Says Devane: "When I made the net eagle on 15, I turn around, Raymond high-fives me, and the next thing I know Tiger's high-fiving me. "Nice putt, dude!" That went right down till the end. It was great. I'm into winning, so I really enjoyed myself."

*D*evane had a bit of an advantage in the Lexus because he's a member at the course. Actually, it's one of the eight courses he can play in the desert, where he lives and also owns an eponymous restaurant. As a member of PGA West, which has five fabulous courses, he only has to pay an additional $200 a month in dues to play the three first-rate courses at the La Quinta Resort. "It's a terrific deal," he says. "It's $225 just to play the resort's Mountain Course once as a nonmember. So I can choose from eight great courses. There's not a lousy course there."

Devane, who picked up the game ten years ago when he came to the desert to play polo, tees it up often with his two sons, Josh, a 3-handicap, and Jake, who manages to shoot in the 80s despite infrequent play. He gets out as often as five times a week when he's not working, enjoying the constant challenge the game provides. "I like just trying to keep myself under control," he says. "My younger son, Jake, is a natural athlete. You tell him one thing and he can build on that in two seconds. You could tell me one thing and I could go a mile backward."

*D*evane has hit a lot of memorable shots over the years, but nothing even comes close to a putt he made at the 1997 AT&T Pebble Beach National Pro-Am. He and pro partner Roger Maltbie started the third round on the 10th hole at Poppy Hills Golf Course. They were right on the bubble of making the cut when they came to their final hole, the 508-yard par-5 9th. Just on the right front edge of the huge green in four, Devane was left with a ninety-foot putt for par with about forty-five feet of break. The hole, located back left, was a good ten feet above his head. Maltbie, who was standing up by the hole, was just hoping the actor could get down in two.

"I hit it dead straight up the hill and then it started breaking left," Devane recalls. "It was funny, because twenty feet from the hole Maltbie started running toward me. He knew it was going to go in. It was the greatest putt in the history of the world. He said you could stand there for five years with a bucket of balls and never even get it close."

The miracle putt, however, wasn't captured on video. The cameras had just packed up and left before the pair arrived. But the par net birdie allowed them to make the cut, getting Devane the coveted umbrella with the AT&T logo and "I MADE THE CUT" in big letters on it. "That's all anybody is struggling for. Nobody makes the cut. There are only twenty-five players. Ties don't even make it. They card out the ties. It's the best moment in golf for me ever."

Tom Dreesen

Comedian Tom Dreesen fell in love with the game as a poor kid from South Chicago caddying for gangsters. Now he gets paid to play the game as one of the founding members of the Celebrity Players Tour, which holds about eight tournaments a year with an average purse of $200,000. "I'm the leading money winner on tour among stand-up comedians," he says. "Of course, I'm the only stand-up comedian, although Dan Quayle's on the tour, so there might be two of us."

In his youth, Dreesen caddied two bags a day, every day. "I had eight brothers and sisters," he says. "We lived in a shack. Five of us slept in a bed. We had no bathtub and no shower or hot water. I had holes in my shoes as big and round as a coffee cup my whole childhood. If someone would have pulled me aside when I was a little boy and said, 'One day, when you grow up, they're going to pay you to play golf,' I'd have thought I died and went to heaven."

Dreesen toured for thirteen years as Frank Sinatra's opening act, but he never got the chance to play golf with him, since

Sinatra had given up the game by then. "He loved the game," Dreesen says. "He was about a 15-handicap, but he quit playing—in my opinion, because he couldn't perfect it, and Sinatra's a perfectionist. This game is so frustrating, and not to be able to master something frustrated him."

He did get the chance to play with Sammy Davis Jr., however, when he opened for Davis in the 1970s. "Sammy was about a 20-handicap," Dreesen recalls. "He didn't hit it far, but he hit it straight. He had a golf cart that had a television set, it had a mini-bar, video-tapes. He had a *barber* in the thing. You'd be getting ready to hit the ball and you'd hear 'Don-da-don-da-DON-NA,' and he's watching *Bonanza* on the golf course. I've never seen a cart like it in my life."

*D*reesen's favorite tournament on the celebrity tour is the Isuzu Celebrity Golf Championship, which is held each July in Lake Tahoe. "It's our Masters," says the comedian, a 5-handicap whose best score came in 1996 when he shot a 1-over-par 73 after double-bogeying the first hole. Another memorable round occurred his first year playing in the event in 1989, when he carded his worst score, an 88. He was playing with Frankie Avalon and former Oakland Raiders football player Fred Williamson.

On the par-3 5th, Avalon ballooned his tee shot up in the air. "I teed up my ball and was getting ready to hit, and his ball was still in the air," Dreesen recounts. "Just before I swung, I said, 'Damn, Frankie, what the hell did you hit there?' He said, 'Six-iron.' And Williamson screams out, 'That's a two-stroke penalty on both you guys. You're not supposed to ask advice and you're not supposed to respond.' He could have warned us. That upset me, because I didn't do it purposely. It was an inadvertent thing. It was a real chickenshit call. Jack Nicklaus told me he'd seen the broadcast and said it's never been called on the PGA Tour. The caddies signal each other all over the place. The players will walk back and show you what they hit. You've still got to hit the shot."

Clint Eastwood

*I*n *Dirty Harry*, Clint Eastwood says, "A man has got to know his
limitations." He could have been referring to his golf game.
Though the squinty-eyed legend has been playing golf for more than
thirty years, the strength he has exhibited on-screen in his long film
career never really translated to the golf course. "As a golfer, he's not
what we'd call the Dirty Harry of the links," says Eddie Merrins,
longtime head pro at Bel-Air Country Club, where Eastwood is a
member and plays to a 15-handicap. "He doesn't hit the ball as far as
you would think. But he has a knack for scoring and a lot of finesse."

Eastwood, who owns the film rights to Michael Murphy's *Golf in
the Kingdom*, plays most of his golf in northern California in Carmel,
where he was the mayor from 1985 to '88, and is now building a golf
course community called Canada Woods. The actor is as much a fixture in the Monterey area as the AT&T Pebble Beach National Pro-
Am, which he played in for twenty-two straight years, starting in
1965, with pro Raymond Floyd.

"We weren't great at making the cut," Floyd says. "I think we
made it three times. When I think about Clint and golf, I think of
my wife, Maria, and me staying with him at his house. He'd play the
piano from time to time. It was always a wonderful week. We have
a very close friendship even now, and it all stems from the game of
golf."

Clint Eastwood, Lexus Challenge, La Quinta, California, 1997

Eastwood hadn't been playing very long when he and Floyd were first paired together. "He didn't have a lot of time for golf," Floyd says. "When he had free time, he skied more. But as time went on he became a member at Cypress Point, got to like the game more, and became a much better player."

Though Eastwood would play to an 18-handicap those first few years, he wasn't "an accomplished 18," says Floyd, who didn't try to give Clint too many pointers. "I'm not one to meddle. I let a guy play. If you start giving him lessons in the middle of a round, he becomes totally confused. That's why Clint and I got along so well. I wasn't one of these lesson givers. Some pros will drive you crazy for eighteen holes telling you what you did wrong."

Perhaps the funniest moment occurred in the late 1960s when they were paired with pro Al Besselink and former Dodgers pitcher Don Drysdale. They had reached the top of the 8th fairway at Pebble Beach and were preparing to hit across the chasm to the green, the approach Jack Nicklaus calls "the greatest second shot in golf."

"It was a very wet year," Floyd recounts, "and Don took a fairway wood to hit it across. Clint and I were standing off to the side of him to watch him hit the shot. He takes this great big backswing. He came down hard on it, and at contact you automatically swing your head up to follow the ball. But with my peripheral vision, I see this ball and it's going backwards. He had hit down on it with the sole plate of this 3-wood and drove it down into the ground. The spin that he imparted on it made it spit back out, and it went about five yards straight behind him. Clint and I were laughing so hard, we were down on our knees. It was really a fun moment."

Douglas Fairbanks

D ouglas Fairbanks was not only responsible for introducing most of Hollywood to the Riviera Country Club when it opened in 1927; he also helped bring professional golf to the club, according to *The Riviera Country Club: A Definitive History*, by Geoff Shackelford. (His wife, screen legend Mary Pickford, was a devoted golfer as well, and she donated some of the club's first trophies.) Riviera was then, as now, an extremely tough test, and Fairbanks was concerned that golfers weren't shooting low enough scores. (So difficult was it that after Bobby Jones shot 73 on the course the first time he played it, he remarked, "Fine course, but tell me, where do the members play?")

Fairbanks offered a $1,000 purse for touring pros who could break par during a three-day stretch prior to the 1928 Los Angeles Open at El Caballero Country Club. He offered $100 for a 70, $200 for a 69, $300 for a 68, and $400 for a 67. Fairbanks's money was safe; no one broke par. Later that year, he also established an open stroke-play tournament so that "Eastern players and the best in the West can test their skill on a course that needs only time and touch of familiarity to become as famous as Pine Valley and other European courses."

Fairbanks was also instrumental in bringing the Los Angeles Open to Riviera in 1929, putting up $1,000 of the record $10,000 purse. The rest of the money came from the first $100-a-plate dinner ever held in the United States, according to the Shackelford book.

Will Rogers was the master of ceremonies. He opened the evening by pulling a $100 bill from his pocket, handed it to tournament chairman Durwood Howes, then told the audience that he, too, was paying his hundred dollars "like all the rest of you suckers!"

The tournament was won by Macdonald Smith. The favorite, Walter Hagen, was never in it after an opening-round 77 and an introduction on the first tee by actress Fay Ward as "the Opium Champion of Great Britain!"

W. C. Fields

William Claude Fields was quite an active golfer, both on the course and on the screen. Moviegoers first heard Fields's distinctive voice in *The Golf Specialist*, a collection of his classic Ziegfeld Follies stage routines released in 1930 (all his films before that were silent). He also appeared in a number of Bobby Jones's instructional shorts, most of which were shot at Lakeside Golf Club, where Fields played most of his golf. He was a decent golfer who usually shot in the high 80s.

He was also quite a character. One day at the club in the mid-1940s, according to Lakeside's fiftieth-anniversary book, Fields took a mighty swing on the first tee and said, "Saaaaay, one of my better drives," even though he actually whiffed the ball. Last to hit in his foursome, Fields strutted off the tee down the fairway, as his caddie, George "Scorpy" Doyle, scooped up the ball. Fields stopped in the middle of the fairway about 150 yards out and declared, "A great drive must be around here somewhere—look, caddie, look." Scorpy took the ball out of his pocket, placed it on a good lie and said, "Here it is, Mr. Fields."

*F*ields used to live right across the lake from the club. "You could see him many Sunday mornings," recalled Roger Kelly, eleven times Lakeside's club champion. "He'd come out with a damn cane in his hand [in his pajamas], raising hell with the ducks. They were up on the lawn, quacking away, and he'd be chasing them in his own inimitable fashion. He'd never get them. He'd holler at them, swing at them, swear at them. This one Sunday morning, his sliding doors open, he comes charging out again. We figure, 'Here we go again, boys! Here comes our show.' This time he didn't have the cane. He had a damn shotgun and he shot every one of them. He said, 'That'll teach you.'"

Dennis Franz

*D*etective Andy Sipowicz plays to a 14-handicap when he's not collaring criminals on *NYPD Blue*. But it was another police character Dennis Franz made famous, Norman Buntz on *Hill Street Blues*, who sent an inebriated crowd into a frenzy during the pro-am of the Greater Greensboro Open not long after the show ended its six-year run in 1987. "There was a par 3 that had a reputation of being a rowdy hole," says the actor, who's been playing golf for seventeen years. "It was near the concession stand, and as the day progressed the fans got rowdier and rowdier from all the beer. I had reached the green on my tee shot, but I had to be forty feet away. As I walked up they all started chanting, 'Buntz, Buntz.' They were waving, having a good time. I got over the putt and there was a big hush. Everyone was very polite. It was dead silent. I stopped in the middle of my backswing, looked up, and said, 'So what are you all so quiet about now?' And with that, they started screaming."

So what does Franz do? He drains the forty-footer and the crowd goes crazy again, shouting "Buntz! Buntz!"—which is a lot easier to say than Sipowicz, especially after a few beers.

*P*erhaps the worst time Franz ever had on the golf course occurred in 1986 when he first played in the latest incarnation of the Crosby, held at Bermuda Run Country Club in North Carolina. "I was so thrilled that I was invited," he says. "It was like a fantasy for me to be able to play in the Crosby. I went there and practiced. I thought I had a relatively good game, not realizing the impact of all the spectators, how it was going to affect me."

A big gallery, gathered around the first tee, applauded his name after the announcer blared it out. Franz couldn't have been more excited if they had just called his name to win an Oscar. "I was so nervous, I pulled a President Ford," he says. "I winged one right into the audience. It's a miracle that it didn't hit anybody. I just toed it and it did a beeline off to the right and ran into the crowd. Major slice."

Since he hit it out-of-bounds, Franz had to hit another ball and endure more embarrassment. "I popped that one about twenty yards up in the air and twenty yards out. It was total humiliation. I went from my greatest high to my greatest depths. I'm happy to say that the game improved from that point on, but that was low."

Peter Gallagher

*T*he costar of such films as *sex, lies and videotape* and *While You Were Sleeping*, Peter Gallagher is an 18-handicap who belongs to Pelham Country Club, near New York City, where Gene Sarazen outlasted Walter Hagen for the 1923 PGA Championship. He got hooked the first time he played ten years ago with borrowed clubs on a Los Angeles municipal course.

"I remember the first hole I played," he says. "I was in a sand trap taking practice swings just covering the green with sand. My buddy looked at me and said, 'What the fuck are you doing?' I said, 'Taking practice swings.' He goes, 'You don't do that in a bunker.' 'Well, you do it everywhere else.' So this is where I was starting out from. I just loved it, even though I didn't have a clue."

It was Jack Lemmon who gave Gallagher his first set of clubs and really got him playing when they were making the 1988 TV movie *The Murder of Mary Phagan* in Richmond, Virginia. Like postal workers, neither rain nor sleet nor gloom of night kept them from their appointed rounds. "We played all the time," Gallagher recalls. "Once, we were the only two people out on the course, and it was raining so hard. We were crazy to be out there. There was thunder and lightning. We came to this little par 3 over water, and Jack's club went flying out of his hand because it was so wet. It went sailing in a perfect arc right in the middle of the pond. Just the butt was sticking up about an inch above water. He looked at me and said, 'Well?'

I said, 'All right, all right, I'll get it.' I take my shoes off, which was ridiculous because they were soaked anyway. I had shorts on, and I wade in and grabbed the club. We didn't quite finish the round, but afterward I'm telling the guys in the pro shop about the golf club and they said, 'Man, you are lucky to be alive. Do you have any idea how many water moccasins are out there?' The place was crawling with poisonous snakes."

Gallagher played the AT&T Pebble Beach National Pro-Am for the first time in 1997 with pro Dan Pohl, finishing 23 under par and just missing the cut by a shot, which he was kind of relieved about because he didn't want to have to tell Lemmon, who has struggled to make the cut for twenty-five years. It was one of the greatest times of his life, even if he did almost drown Tom Kite with a glob of mud on the practice range.

His finest moment came when he played at Spyglass Hill Golf Course. He had hit yet another drive to the right in the woods on a par 5. "The only way out was through two trees that made a V about twelve yards in the front of the ball," he recalls. "The widest part was about three feet wide. I was thinking, 'I got to get it through that V,' when Dan came up to me and said, 'What are you going to do?' I said, 'I'm thinking of hitting the 5-iron.' He said, 'Hit the 4-iron.' He handed me my 4-iron and left. I put it back and I take out the 5-iron. For whatever reason I hit one of the best shots in my life. It went screaming straight through the V about 180 yards. It landed in a perfect spot just short of a lake, right where I had been aiming. And I heard this guy behind me say, 'He's no 18!' That was the best moment for me. I thought, 'Isn't it great to be thought of as a sandbagger? Isn't that a compliment?'"

Gallagher recently made a film in London, *The Man Who Knew Too Little*, with Bill Murray, and the two played half a dozen times at the famed Wentworth golf club. One match ended in darkness. "We were going into the 18th hole and it was literally pitch black at this point," Gallagher recalls. "It was a long par 4, and right around where your drive lands there were a bunch of fairway bunkers. Bill's ball landed in the fairway and mine ended up in one of the bunkers. His second shot ended just left of the green but far from the hole."

Gallagher had to play sideways out of the bunker with a sand wedge just to get back to the fairway, where he had a *Golf in the Kingdom*–like epiphany as he prepared to hit his 150-yard approach. "I remember thinking this: 'Here I am in England. It's pitch black, I can barely see the ball on the ground, much less where it's going to go. I can see from the horizon an idea of where the pin is, but it's really dark so I don't think I'll even find this ball.'"

He hit one of the best shots of his life. "It was one of those things where you just let the force be with you," he says. "You're relaxed because you know there's very little else you can do. Plus, it was kind of exciting, because I've never played in such darkness. I swung and made good contact. I had no idea where it went, but I just had a feeling. I knocked it four feet from the hole. Bill chips to about the same distance, and being the competitive master that he is, he sinks the putt and I don't, so he took me. I said, 'Oh, this is what you need. More of my money.' I remember constantly giving him money on the golf course."

Andy Garcia

*A*ndy Garcia has given a lot of great performances in such films as *The Godfather, Part III* and *When a Man Loves a Woman*, but it was his role as a single-digit player at the 1997 AT&T Pebble Beach National Pro-Am that really got people talking. Garcia, you see, is really about a 16-handicap who had never broken 80 at his home course, Lakeside Golf Club. But he played like a top amateur at the AT&T, contributing 32 shots to the winning score of 43-under posted by himself and his pro partner, Paul Stankowski.

"I don't care what anybody says, I'm not a sandbagger," Garcia said after breaking the all-time scoring record in the pro-am division. "But I know how it looks." He attributed his Oscar-caliber performance to Stankowski, the golfing equivalent of famed Method acting coach Stanislavski, after he helped him with his rhythm and putting.

Though scores aren't kept on every hole for amateurs (just the best team figure), *Golf World* magazine estimated he shot in the 70s in two of the four rounds, at Poppy Hills and Pebble Beach. The USGA's director of handicapping, Dean Knuth, said the odds of someone with Garcia's handicap doing that are less than one in 10,000. But Stankowski stood by his man. "He's a 16 who has the ability to play to single digits," he said. "Andy played really well but showed during every round that he's a legitimate 16. The second day [at Poppy Hills] we were the first off the [10th] tee—nobody was out there—and he shot 36, but on our back nine, with the galleries, he shot 45. Even on Sunday [when he played twelve holes in 3 over par], he had enough [bad holes] to play to about a 14. If he sandbagged, we would have won by fifteen shots. I defend him one hundred percent."

James Garner

One of the best celebrities to ever play the game is James Garner, a longtime Bel-Air Country Club member who was once a scratch player. He's now about a 6-handicap, even though he has trouble getting through the ball because his knees are shot from doing a lot of his own stunts in all those Westerns.

He and singer Mac Davis often tee it up together. Their motto is they play any day that ends in *Y*. "He's one of the most amazing men I've ever seen," Davis says. "He's had every bone in his body broken, he's in pain all the time. In the last ten years, he's had several operations, but within a couple of weeks he's back shooting in the 70s."

Garner's golf philosophy can best be described by the term *positive negativity*. "He gets negative on purpose to make himself play better. That's his deal," Davis says. "He becomes a curmudgeon on the golf course, but a lovable curmudgeon. One time about five years ago, he and I were partners and he was complaining, 'I can't putt anymore, I can't make anything, I'm tired of this.' I've just won a couple of holes in a row and we've got these guys turned around on the bet so that we're 0 and 2 coming up the 18th hole. Jim knocks it four feet from the hole. I just leaned over and I said, 'Jim, quit complaining. You knock this little birdie in here, we turn everything around and we win money for the day.' He says, 'Oh, I can't putt anymore.' I said, 'Jim, for once think positively in your life.' He says, 'Okay, I'm positive I can't make it.'"

After coaxing it in, Garner's mood brightened considerably. He immediately started saying, "Love to putt. Born to putt."

Vince Gill

Country star Vince Gill could give Jack Wagner of *Melrose Place* a run for the title of Best Hollywood Golfer. He's a 2-handicap who plays just about every day. He even has his own tournament, the Vinny, which benefits junior golf in his home state of Tennessee. "I like that you never figure it out," says Gill, whose best round is a 66 at his home course, the Golf Club of Tennessee, near Nashville. "You never get it right. You hit a good one then hit a bad one then a good one. That's the beauty of the game. No matter how much you play you never master it."

Gill has played all the great courses in the country—Augusta, Cypress Point, Pine Valley—but it's the first course he played as a kid growing up in Oklahoma that sticks in his mind most (to call the nine-holer a cow pasture would be insulting to cows). "The greens were made of cotton-seed hulls," he recalls. "They're not too different from sand. You take this big heavy rolling pin four feet wide and roll it across the middle of the green. They had a string attached to the flagstick, so wherever you hit it on the green, you took this string, stretched it around to create a little trough and you'd putt down that."

*T*hough Gill once made a hole in one at the TPC of Scottsdale's rowdy 16th hole during the pro-am of the Phoenix Open (winning a young couple a $175,000 house), his favorite shot is a putt made by good friend Heather Farr, an LPGA pro who died of breast cancer in 1993. They were paired together in a skins game that was part of the Sara Lee Classic, an LPGA Tour event near Nashville. "It was one of the last times she played golf, and she wasn't very healthy," Gill recalls. "We were very close. We were playing against all the big dogs, and nobody thought we'd win a skin. On the first hole, I hit a 7-iron in there to about five feet and she made the putt. It's a very special memory."

Jackie Gleason, Bel-Air Country Club, 1955

Jackie Gleason

Bing Crosby wasn't the only celebrity with his name on a golf tournament. From 1972 to 1980, Jackie Gleason hosted a PGA Tournament at Inverrary Country Club in Fort Lauderdale, Florida, where he was also a member. Gleason, a 15-handicap who played just about every day when he wasn't working, lived right next to the club and used to drive his Rolls-Royce golf cart to the course. Even though he passed away in 1987, Gleason's presence is still very much felt. The club uses his cart to ferry brides to on-course ceremonies.

Sam Snead recalls playing an exhibition with Gleason in Shawnee, Delaware, against fellow pro Art Wall and band leader Fred Waring, who parred the first four holes. "Look at this," a disbelieving Snead told Gleason, who responded, "Don't worry about a thing, boy. All four wheels will come off, even the spare."

"He was right," Snead says. "We ended up winning the match. Jackie got in one trap and holed out from the bunker. He walked off the green up to the next tee, hit his drive, and started to walk. He said, 'My God, I forgot my horse. I'm so shook up from holing that shot.' That night he drank two bottles of champagne and passed out on the course. It took six men to load him into a pickup truck."

*G*leason loved the game so much that he moved his long-running CBS variety show to Miami from New York in 1964 so he could play golf year-round. He even incorporated the game into his work. One of the classic episodes of *The Honeymooners* was called "The Golfer," which first aired on October 15, 1955. Hoping to curry favor with his golf-playing boss to win a promotion to assistant traffic manager, Gleason gives him the impression that he's a champion-caliber player. Of course, he's never touched a club in his life and he's left in a state of panic when his boss invites him to play. With Art Carney reading from an instruction book, Gleason, dressed in plaid knickers and an argyle sweater, has to learn to play golf almost overnight in his drab apartment using a pincushion for a ball. "I can't learn to play golf in two days," Gleason frets. "It'd take me at least a week."

The episode is a real hoot, especially when Carney and Gleason try to figure out what the book means by "address the ball." "I think I know what it means," says Carney as he steps up to the ball, gives a backhanded salute, and shouts, "Hello, ball!" Suffice it to say, Gleason didn't get the promotion.

*I*n his golf memoir, *Confessions of a Hooker*, Bob Hope revealed how much Gleason liked to gamble on the course. "The first time we played, for $100 a hole, he took me pretty good," Hope wrote. "But I got so I could beat him nearly every time."

One time during the pro-am at Jack Nicklaus's Memorial Tournament in Ohio, Gleason and Hope came to the short par-4 14th with a $1,000 carryover. Gleason made the green in three, while Hope didn't get on till his fourth shot after going bunker to bunker. Gleason three-putted for a 6 and Hope made his putt for a 5. "I tapped him for about $1,400 that day, which almost got me even with him for the year," Hope recalled. "After a while we started to pay off after each hole, because we tended to get our score and our finances confused. We'd whip out the money on the next tee, much to the delight of the gallery."

Robert Goulet

Singer Robert Goulet hasn't played much golf the last couple of years because of a bad hip and back, but he used to play to about a 10-handicap and even won the pro-am portion of the Bob Hope Desert Classic one year in the seventies. He also played many times in Bing Crosby's Clambake at Pebble Beach, where he was paired with the late Dave Marr one year. It was a typical Monterey day— rain and forty-mph winds. On the short par-4 4th at Pebble, Goulet ended up in the fairway bunker while Marr was way left, leaving him a shot into the teeth of the gale. Under calm conditions, Marr would have hit half a wedge, but on this day he needed something like a 5-iron.

"As he hit it, I said, 'Oh, my God, he sculled it,'" Goulet recalls. "The ball went over the green toward the gallery standing on a mound behind it. They ducked as the ball went over their heads. Through the rain I could see the ball going out to the ocean. Then, all of a sudden, it was being picked up and wafted back toward the people. The gallery on the mound ducked a second time. It just missed a trap, bounced on the green twice, and went into the hole for a deuce. He's a Texas player, so he knew about wind. He knew he had to hit it low and hard because the wind was going to bring it back. I looked at him and said, 'How about that!' He just said, 'Yeah, yeah.' Those tour pros are all so humble about their great shots."

*F*our years ago Goulet was playing in a pro-am with Lee Trevino at the Desert Inn in Las Vegas, where he lives. "I'm a Christian and I pray to God, but I don't ever ask him for anything," the entertainer says. "I just asked for this one thing: 'Please, Lord, just let me get off the first tee.' I prayed for two months, for the last month, the last two weeks, the last three days to get off the tee. We get on the tee, there are ten thousand people around us because they all love Lee. Lee hits first. Bang, straight out. We're joking and laughing and everything is fabulous. I'm the high handicapper, so the low handicapper gets up, hits one, bang, okay, more laughs. The second handicapper hits, bang, more laughs. Then Lee said, 'Bob, are you going to hit a ball?' I had the ball resting on a tee in my hand. All I had to do was put the tee in the ground. I've been nervous before for opening nights on Broadway and singing for presidents and the Queen of England, but this was nervous. My hands were almost shaking."

As he stuck the tee in the ground, the ball started to teeter, and Goulet said to himself, "If that ball falls off, I'm leaving." It settled down. After running through a laundry list of preswing checkpoints that would make a space shuttle countdown seem rushed by comparison, Goulet noticed a deafening silence. "No one was making a sound. I finally said, 'How long have I been here? Five minutes, ten minutes, an hour?' I finally hit it and it went thirty feet into the scrub brush right in front of me. I looked up and I said, 'Thank you, Lord.' You don't ask for things. Even though the Bible says, 'Ask and you shall receive,' I didn't receive. The Lord doesn't give you those silly little things. He'll give you the big things."

Amy Grant, Bob Hope Chrysler Classic, Indian Wells, California, 1997

Amy Grant

*T*here are snakes in golf, and then there are *snakes*. Anyone who's played the game has had a snake, or three-putt, but country star Amy Grant has had to do battle with the real thing from time to time. The 21-handicap belongs to the Golf Club of Tennessee, near Nashville. The Tom Fazio course is basically cut out of the wilderness, so it has a heavy snake population. Not long after she started playing four years ago she was getting ready to putt when a poisonous copperhead slithered up beside her.

"It was a little one, so I just cleated it to death," she says proudly. "It was before the club went spikeless. It scared me. I felt like I had to deal with it right there. I stepped on it several times. It was just a bad snake year at our golf club, but I'm a farm girl so I'm used to it."

Her husband, Gary Chapman, carries a sawed-off shotgun in his golf bag. "It's called a snake charmer. I used to carry a knife in my golf bag," says Grant, who feels lucky to get out once every ten days with three kids at home and a full-time job. "My mom, Gloria, has always loved it and now that all her kids are grown, she gets to enjoy it a lot. I keep going, 'Well, someday I'm gonna really start playing more.'"

A country girl who spends lots of time inside windowless recording studios and dark theaters, Grant loves that the game gets her outside. "I also love the pace of it," says the singer, whose best round is an 86. "It's just kind of methodical and slow. But my favorite thing is the people that you meet playing golf. You can have the most unlikely pairings of people. And then you've got four hours to talk— or not talk. I've played with so many men and women that I never would have met except on a golf course. I've played whole rounds with people and not until the 18th hole will they say, 'Hey, we really like your music.' Whenever anybody recognizes me, though, I think, 'Oh, God, how bad did I lose my temper? Did I throw a club?'"

A multiple Grammy winner who's sold close to 20 million records, Amy has had a lot of hits in her day but there's one she'd rather forget. She was on an adjoining hole and was hit in the stomach when some guy hooked his drive. "It knocked me down," she says. "Everybody came rushing over." Fortunately, she was OK, but not so the guy who beaned her. Can you imagine the look on his face when he found out he just took out Amy Grant?

Bryant Gumbel

Perhaps no celebrity is as obsessed with the game as former *Today* show cohost Bryant Gumbel, now with CBS News. To wit: he belongs to four (count 'em, *four*) country clubs—Waccabuc (across the street from his home in New York's Westchester County), Burning Tree (a male-only club near Washington, D.C., where George Bush sponsored his membership), Hudson National (one of the most exclusive clubs in New York), and Whipporwhill in Armonk, New York (where he plays the most).

"I enjoy everything about the game," says Gumbel, who started playing eighteen years ago and is now a 7-handicap. "I enjoy the camaraderie, I enjoy being alone out here. It's a place where you can get away from the rest of the world. I enjoy the singular sense of achievement or failure. In golf, whatever you do, you did."

Gumbel plays about 150 times a year, and of all his rounds, the most memorable came in 1994 when Johnny Miller, his partner at the AT&T Pebble Beach National Pro-Am, won the event even though he had basically been retired since 1987. "If you play in the finals of a pro event and you're the last group and you play with the coleaders, that's hard to beat," recalls Gumbel, who scored in the mid-80s on national TV. "It's hard to say exactly what I shot, because you pick up rather than hold up the leaders, but I played pretty decent that day. It was a lot of fun."

Bryant Gumbel, Isuzu Celebrity Golf Championship, Lake Tahoe, 1997

His joy isn't diminished by the fact that he was responsible for one of the stranger events in PGA Tour history. In the final round, on a wet and windy day, Miller came to the par-3 17th at Pebble tied for the lead with Tom Watson. Up ahead on the green, Watson three-putted from thirty-five feet to give Miller a one-shot lead as Gumbel prepared to tee off. Hitting into the wind, Gumbel took a pretty good whack at the ball. You might say he even killed it. He launched the ball smack dab into a seagull that was flying in front of the tee, killing the bird and the tee shot.

"I'm sitting on the tee and I see Watson miss his putt," Miller said afterward. "I have a one-shot lead. I'm seeing the surf beating up on those rocks out there, it's a tough pin, and I've got the wrong club. It was like, 'What can I do to overcome this?' Then Bryant hit the seagull and killed it right in front of us. It was sad. I had to get all that out of my system."

Miller parred the hole to go on and win the tournament, of course, while Gumbel ended up with a birdie, but not the kind he would have liked.

While Gumbel's best round is a 71, which he shot a few different ent times, some of his worst rounds have come at the Isuzu Celebrity Championship, held each July at Edgewood golf course in Lake Tahoe. At the 1997 tournament, he shot 94 the first day. (He salvaged it somewhat the next day when he shot an 86 and he and Marcus Allen won $1,000 each from Charles Barkley and Seth Joyner.) The 94 was a full nine shots better than one of his rounds three years earlier in the same tournament. Incredibly, he shot 103 while making nine pars.

"I had five 8s and four 7s," he says matter-of-factly. "I just had mental breakdowns. People don't understand—when they see us shoot 86, they think, 'I can do better than that.' But they don't realize, that's giving themselves putts, that's when they hit one out-of-bounds and say, 'Give me a 6 and walk away.' It's hard to do it when you're playing your own ball all the way up."

Gumbel has no pretensions about trying to play on the Senior Tour or even winning the club championship at one of his four clubs. "I would just like to be consistent in competition and shoot like I do back home with regularity. Back home I string four rounds together in the 70s every day out. I'd just like to play well and reach the point where I have some degree of consistency."

Don't we all.

Steve Guttenberg

*T*he goofy star of such hits as *Three Men and a Baby*, *Cocoon*, and all those Police Academy movies, Steve Guttenberg has been playing seriously for only a year or so. He was first introduced to the game, however, at thirteen, when he caddied at Bethpage golf course on Long Island, site of the 2002 U.S. Open. Not surprisingly, the 20-handicap had his best round, an 88, when he returned to Bethpage's Blue Course for the first time this past summer.

"It brought back so many memories," says the actor, who used to get $5 for a loop, $7.50 for two bags, and would even caddie in the winter months. "You'd carry around this piece of AstroTurf, and your player hit the ball off the AstroTurf into the snow. It was never a thick snow. You'd spray paint the ball, but you had to keep a good eye on it. Then we'd brush the greens off with a broom. I didn't do it a whole lot because it was all illegal since the golf course was closed."

One winter's day, he was caddying for a gent who was more interested in hitting the bottle than hitting the ball (to help him keep warm, no doubt). While the guy staggered up to the 15th green, Guttenberg carved "Steve G." into a big maple off to the side. He paid a little visit to the tree during his round there last summer. "And, if you can believe it, it's still there twenty-five years later," he says. "It was amazing."

Oliver Hardy

Oliver Hardy, the heavier half of the legendary comedy team, was one of Lakeside Golf Club's "earliest and best-liked members," the club's fiftieth-anniversary book, written by Norman Blackburn, notes. He was about a 20-handicap who thoroughly enjoyed the game. One year, he wound up against actor Adolphe Menjou in the finals of the last flight of the club championship. There was more trash-talking and betting on the match than on a Tyson-Holyfield fight. They each kept postponing the match in hopes of out-practicing the other before the big day. Menjou accused "Babe," as Hardy was called, of ducking him. "I'm at my peak now, and Babe knows it. He's waiting for me to slough off."

"Quite a book developed," Bing Crosby told Blackburn. "When they finally teed off there must have been $6,000 to $7,000 bet on the match. They finally teed off and a hell of a gallery showed up. . . . It was supposed to be eighteen holes, and it took them about seven or eight hours to play. They followed each other into traps and into the rough and needled each other while they hit shots. I think Babe beat him on the last hole. It was a real sensational match. It drew more people than the finals of the club. Everybody had a bet going one way or another, and I don't think either one of them broke 120."

*H*ardy played a lot of golf at the club with W. C. Fields. One day, after hitting his ball in a trap on the 6th hole, Hardy took six or eight whacks at the ball before he finally picked up. "About two weeks later, Babe showed up with a strange-looking club," actor Richard Arlen recounted in the Blackburn book. "Babe's club had a face on it about six inches wide, and it was real heavy. He had it specially made from an old niblick. All you had to do was drop it in the sand trap and the ball would come out and land on the green. Babe was in ecstasy, but Fields was furious and threatened to have him thrown out of the club. He said, 'Any man who would use an illegal club like that would strangle his mother.'"

Katharine Hepburn

K atharine Hepburn, who had a home on the 14th hole at Bel-Air Country Club, was a fine golfer. She liked to play from the men's tees and could shoot in the 80s. She began playing when she was five at a private nine-hole course near her parents' summer home in Fenwick, Connecticut, and took lessons as a teenager. In 1938, just hours before that year's great hurricane ravaged the New England coast, she made a hole-in-one at Fenwick's 9th.

After moving to Los Angeles to pursue a movie career, she often played with the head of RKO pictures, Howard Hughes. Eddie Gannon, Lakeside's starter, caddied for her one day when she played with Hughes. "They played eighteen holes in about two hours," he recalls. "They were both very fast walkers."

In her autobiography, *Me*, she recalled a round with Hughes at Bel-Air. "I was playing golf with the pro and we were about to finish a nine-hole lesson when there was the noise of an airplane. Howard landed practically on top of us. He took his clubs out of the plane and finished the nine with us. Naturally, the club was furious. He had to have a truck come over and virtually dismantle the plane to get rid of it."

What she didn't mention, however, is that Hughes refused to pay the $2,000 turf-repair bill the club sent him. Instead, he offered to donate $5,000 to any charity designated by the club, which he did. The next day he resigned from the club and never set foot on the course again.

*H*epburn played a lot of golf on-screen, too, most notably in the 1952 film *Pat and Mike* with Spencer Tracy. He played her fast-talking manager who shows her off at Riviera Country Club against real-life LPGA stars Babe Zaharias, Betty Hicks, and Helen Dettweiler in a tournament called the Women's National Match Play Championship. And it's clear that it's Katharine the Great herself who does all the golfing. There was no stand-in. She hits twenty-four shots, including one from casual water, one from the woods, and two from bunkers. In one scene, demonstrating to an old busybody how good she really is, she hits nine teed-up balls on a practice range in about ten seconds.

Bob Hope, Palm Springs, California, 1967

Bob Hope

*W*ith his omnipresent driver during his comedy routines and his love of the game, Bob Hope has done probably as much to help make the game popular as Arnold Palmer. The Bob Hope Desert Classic, a ninety-hole birdie bonanza, has carried his name since 1965. The event has attracted more celebrities over the years than the Academy Awards.

Hope got hooked on the game in 1930 while on the vaudeville circuit. At his best, in the early fifties, he played to a 6. "Golf is my real profession," he wrote in his 1985 golf memoir, *Confessions of a Hooker*. "Entertainment is just a sideline. I tell jokes to pay my greens fees."

He wasn't bad at hustling a bet, either. "He was the best match maker," recalls eleven-time Lakeside club champion Roger Kelly. "He'd plead for extra strokes, then, at the turn, he'd be up and he wouldn't make an adjustment. You'd say, 'You've got to cut back to what it should be.' 'No, no, you get out the way you got in.'"

*H*ope, whose home—with a practice hole in the backyard—is just five minutes away from Lakeside Golf Club, didn't play for much money. His usual bet was a $10 nassau, except when he played with Del Webb, the industrialist who built Sun City in Arizona. Their standard game was for $25 with a variety of side bets and double or nothing on the 18th hole. One day at Lakeside, Hope was up $875 when they came to the double-or-nothing 18th, a 400-yard par 4.

"We both hit good drives," Hope recounts in his book. "On my second shot I hooked a 4-wood just left of the green and a little short. Del was on the front edge of the green with a 3-iron. I was going to hit a wedge for my third, but I switched to a 9-iron and rolled it into the cup for a birdie-3. Del, who hardly ever swore, glowered at me and said, 'Hope, you sonuvabitch!' I got him for over $1,700."

*H*ope, of course, played a lot of golf with Bing Crosby, whom he met in 1932 in New York when they were winding down their vaudeville days and doing three or four shows a day at the Capitol Theater. They used to hit balls between shows at a driving range under the 59th Street Bridge.

The Capitol is where they developed their patter that became the basis of their seven *Road* movies. While making *Road to Utopia* (1945), they were caught playing at Lakeside when they should have been meeting with the costumer, who had to get two suits ready for the next day's shoot. The producer, Paul Jones, threw a fit—literally. With the wardrobe department in tow, Jones caught them on the 4th tee. Out came the yellow tape measure, and a fitting took place right on the tee as other groups played through.

Howard Hughes

*I*t's easy to see why Howard Hughes became a recluse. He was hiding from golf. The man was consumed with it. He wanted to be as good as Bobby Jones but couldn't quite get there. Hughes was a scratch golfer who took a lot of lessons from Riviera pro and 1921 British Amateur champion Willie Hunter. He would often bring a cameraman or two from his studio, RKO, to film his swing, then he and Hunter would study the swing in a private screening room back on the lot.

One day Hughes asked Hunter, a blunt-speaking Scotsman, if he had the potential to become the U.S. Amateur champion. "No, Howard," replied Hunter. "You don't." With that, Hughes put his clubs away and rarely, if ever, picked them up again.

"He wanted to be number one, and he trusted my dad," says Mac Hunter, who succeeded his father at Riviera in 1964. "When he was told he couldn't be the best, he didn't want any part of it."

A Lakeside Golf Club member, Hughes often played there with former U.S. Amateur champion George Von Elm. The two played for $500 a match two or three times a week, with Von Elm winning almost every time. One time, though, Hughes played really well and won. As Von Elm wrote out a check, he started to complain about all the bad breaks he had and said Hughes was lucky.

Von Elm ended up losing a lot more than $500. "He was bitching and griping about it to the point that Hughes said, 'I'm never going to play with you again,'" recalls Lakeside's longtime starter, Eddie Gannon. With that, Hughes ripped up the check and Von Elm lost tens of thousands of dollars he no doubt would have won in future bets.

*T*wo of Hughes's regular partners at the club were film director Dave Butler and good friend Jim Oviatt. After Hughes and another member lost to Butler and Oviatt, Butler collected his $40 from their fourth. Hughes was so angry with his play that he headed straight to the range, where he practiced well into the dark, never settling up his bets.

"Later on in life he made that fantastic solo trip around the world," Butler recalls in Lakeside's fiftieth-anniversary book. "And when he got to Moscow, which was his goal, Jim Oviatt sent him a wire: 'Dear Howard, congratulations on your marvelous feat. Don't forget, you owe me $40.' The next day, Hughes's secretary called Oviatt and said, 'Mr. Hughes telephoned in and wants to know where you want the check sent—to the ranch or the office.'"

Samuel L. Jackson

Samuel L. Jackson is an 18-handicap who's been playing for three years. A member of MountainGate Country Club in Los Angeles, he recently broke 80 for the first time. "I didn't even realize I had broken 80 until I had done it," he says. "I was totally unconscious."

Jackson, who just started his own charity golf tournament, enjoys the game's solitary pursuit. "It's just me and the ball," he says. "It's kind of quiet and Zen-like. I like that you can't play the game with tension. You have to be relaxed to make it work for yourself. And golf courses are very beautiful, serene kind of places to be. It hooked me from the beginning. I try to have fun no matter what happens, 'cause golf changes from day to day. I pick up my clubs some days and they treat me like an enemy. Then I go out there some days and it's almost like I think I'm ready to go on tour."

$H$is favorite memory is the first time he played with his idol, Sidney Poitier, two years ago at Hillcrest Country Club in Los Angeles, where Poitier is a member. "I think Sidney knew I was kind of awed by the fact that I was with him," says Jackson, who shot 86

Samuel L. Jackson, Police-Celebrity Golf Tournament, Los Angeles, 1997

to beat Poitier. "My wife said, 'You weren't supposed to beat him!' I don't think he minded, though. I don't lose to my bosses, either. I just go out there and play. A lot of times I don't even know what the other guys' scores are, even though I have one friend who disappears into the woods, hits the ball eight times, comes out, and says, 'Give me a bogey.'"

Joanna Kerns

*T*he former star of *Growing Pains* and current TV movie-of-the-week queen, Joanna Kerns is a 21-handicap who picked up the game ten years ago. She sees the game as a meta-*fore* for life. "Golf," she says, "is like life, where everything gets in your way." She's so intent on getting better that she'll drive all the way across Los Angeles to take lessons from famed swing guru Mac O'Grady at a public course when her own course, Riviera Country Club, is just five minutes away (the club doesn't allow outside teachers to give instruction).

"He's changed so much, but it's going to make a huge difference if I can incorporate it all," says Kerns, whose brother, Kurt DiVerona, used to play the minitours. "Mac has me loading the wrists, getting a real angle coming into the ball. He's also got me really anchored and centered on the base with a good turn. I have moments where it's really brilliant, then I go right back to where I've been forever."

*K*erns is one of the few female celebrities who plays, so she gets invited to a lot of tournaments. About eight years ago, she was playing one at the Mauna Lani resort in Hawaii where she ended up in a shoot-out with a bunch of guys for two first-class, round-trip tickets to Europe. "I went into it thinking, 'This is a lark. I'll never win them anyway, so I'm going to have a good time.'"

By the 9th hole all other teams except hers and one other had been eliminated. "I was getting ready to chip over a trap onto the green when I heard that this was for the tickets to Europe. And, of course, I looked straight up and my ball dribbled right into the sand trap," recalls Kerns, who came in second. "Once I realized I was in the running, it was all over."

*K*erns plays a lot with another sitcom star and Riviera member, Joe Regalbutto, of *Murphy Brown*. A few years ago, they happened to be in Cabo San Lucas at the same time and Kerns kept calling up Regalbutto's wife, Rosemary, to ask, "Can Joe come out to play with me?" "I wanted to play this Jack Nicklaus course," says the actress, who didn't know Regalbutto's wife very well. "I said, 'Your wife needs to get to know me better so she doesn't think I'm cheating with you.' I don't know what she thought of me."

Greg Kinnear

*F*ormer late-night talk show host turned movie star, Greg Kinnear started playing in his youth, but then his family moved overseas, first to Lebanon and then Greece. "For some reason there was an incredible lack of golf interest in Beirut," he says. "But you really learn how to deal with the trap there."

He picked up the game again in college at the University of Arizona in Tucson, where he played perhaps the worst round of his life at El Conquistador Country Club. "I made the mistake of playing on the day after graduation," says Kinnear, who doesn't remember what he shot. "It was something like 397. It was just a late-night and an early-morning game. It's a recipe for disaster."

Now about a 15-handicap, Kinnear is thinking about joining a club but isn't so sure. "There are so many people I owe games to, I'm going to have to file for bankruptcy just on the guest fees alone," he says.

*H*is best day on the golf course was actually the worst weather-wise. About six years ago he and a couple friends went to the Kapalua Resort on Maui for four days that became "the golf weekend from hell." It had rained for three days straight prior to their arrival, and it would continue every single day while they were there. Finally, by their last day, they had had enough of sitting around drinking mai tais. They were going to play come hell or high water—literally.

"The greens were so immersed in water that in order to hit a three-foot putt, you had to wind up like you were hitting a 5-iron," Kinnear recalls. "You had to swing through with every fiber of your being, and maybe it would go two and a half feet and you'd end up a little short. There were streams coming down the fairway. In the madness of the whole thing, we just said, 'Screw it, we're playing a game of golf here. We will not be denied at least one round.' It turned out to be one of the funniest golfing experiences I ever had. Nothing made sense. The winds were so strong that the ball would fly over your head in the opposite direction. Just to get down in twelve was a miracle, and yet we trotted on. We wouldn't be denied. There is a golf madness that can creep up on any of us, and it hit me in Hawaii."

Cheryl Ladd

*F*ormer *Charlie's Angels* costar Cheryl Ladd is a 17-handicap who plays once or twice a week at her club, Alisal Ranch, in Santa Barbara, when she's not working. "Golf is my game," she says. "I've played a lot of sports, but nothing hooked me like golf. It's an absolutely orgasmic feeling when you hit a ball well because it's so hard."

Her Scottish-born husband, writer-producer Brian Russell, introduced her to the game fifteen years ago. Now all their vacations revolve around golf. "Our children think we're nuts, because it's all we do," Ladd says. "We watch it on TV. We're pretty obsessed."

Unlike most people in Hollywood, Ladd doesn't need therapy. "Golf is my shrink," she says. "I treat it like a Zen thing. You have to clear your mind of everything else to play."

*L*add is one of the few female celebrities who are comfortable enough with their games to play in tournaments. "So I often get to be the token chick, and I mean that in the best sense of the word," she says. Consequently, she's had many memorable moments, such as getting a dual lesson from both Peter Jacobsen and Fred Couples at the 1993 Skins Game at Bighorn Country Club, near Palm Springs.

At the same event, Ladd played with Arnold Palmer in the pro-am. They came to a par 3 that was all desert, tee to green. "There's no 'oops,'" Ladd says. "Your shot is either excellent or awful." Palmer knocked it to within twelve feet of the pin, but then the other three players, all men, sprayed their balls into the desert flora one after the other. Then it was Cheryl's turn to hit as some two hundred members of Arnie's Army ringed the green. The distance: 130 yards; the club: a 5-iron. As she stepped up to the ball all the women in the crowd started cheering and shouting: "C'mon, Cheryl! You can do it!"

Ladd said her "golfer's prayer" ("Lord, give me the strength to hit this ball easy"), took a deep breath, and told herself, "I'm an actress, act like a golfer." She hit it five feet from the pin. "As soon as I gave myself some direction and put myself in that mode, it was a comfortable place to be," says Ladd, who was led onto the green by Palmer, who tipped his hat to her. "To have Arnie applaud your shot, well, I'll never forget it."

A few years ago, Ladd had a hole in one at her home course while playing with her husband and another famous member, tennis legend Jimmy Connors. They were paired together in an impromptu afternoon pickup game on a typically glorious California day. Nobody was on the course. With deer for a gallery, Ladd stepped up to the 122-yard par-3 9th hole with her 6-iron. The ball flew through the air in a perfect parabola at the pin.

"I picked up my tee and turned around because I hit it so well," recalls Ladd, who saw a wide-eyed look on her partners. "Jimmy said, 'Cheryl, it's going in!' I turned around just in time to see it disappear. I was excited, but he was even more excited. He was jumping up and down. Not only had he never had one; he'd never seen one, either."

When they got to the green, Ladd pulled her ball out of the hole while her husband tried to snap a few pictures with her camera for posterity's sake, since the odds of someone getting a hole in one are about one in ten thousand. There was just one problem—no film. She did get a coffee mug from the club, though; it says, "I got a hole in one at the Alisal."

Matt Lauer

*T*he *Today* show cohost is a terrific golfer with a solid swing. His 8-handicap is reflected in the fact that he truly enjoys the game regardless of how he's playing. "When you do what I do for a living, it's a fun job, but it's not the most relaxing," he says. "Golf is four and a half hours of relaxation. Even if I'm playing poorly, I don't forget that I'm spending four and a half hours in what inherently are the most beautiful spots across the country. So what could be wrong with that?"

Lauer learned to play the game from his dad, Jay, who passed away recently. "The most obvious reason I love golf so much is somewhere in the back of my mind when I'm playing the game—it reminds me of the time I spent with my dad out on the course," says Lauer, whose best round was a 73 in front of thousands of fans on the tough Edgewood Tahoe golf course at the 1997 Isuzu Celebrity Championship in Lake Tahoe—his first time ever playing in such a tournament. "I got off to an amazing start. After parring the 1st hole, I birdied the 2nd hole, I birdied the 3rd hole. I lipped out for birdie on the 4th hole, I lipped out for birdie on the 5th hole. I could have been 4 under after five holes. I ended up with five birdies on that day. I went back and forth between 1 over, 1 under, and even, which for me, at my handicap, is a fantasy. I play in member-guest tournaments at clubs, but you don't have galleries out there. You don't have

Matt Lauer, Lexus Challenge, La Quinta, California, 1997

holes with television towers on them, guys holding microphones in the fairway."

When he got back to his hotel after the round, he could barely contain himself. "I was never so pumped up about anything golf-related or sports-related in my life," he says. "I couldn't sleep. I was really pumped up. When I walked through the hallways in the hotel, everybody was saying, 'Nice round, great round.' People don't usually come up to me and say that. It was fun."

There was just one thing missing, however. "There was no one I would rather have called more or first after that round than my dad," Lauer says quietly. "He would have been so thrilled with that round for me."

*L*auer is a member of the Stanwich Club in Greenwich, Connecticut, where he usually gets out about once or twice a week. He also plays a lot with his *Today* show predecessor, Bryant Gumbel. If Matt's not in his anchor chair on Friday, chances are he and Bryant are off on one of their weekend golf trips. It was Bryant, in fact, who was responsible for Matt's second-most-memorable round when he played Pebble Beach for the first time a few years ago.

"We're the first group out," Lauer recalls. "I'm playing with a couple of guys I don't know, and I'm nervous about it, because it's such a great course and you don't want to play poorly. It was one of these perfect Monterey mornings. There's a little mist, it's just starting to lift. There's dew on the grass. It's probably the most beautiful scene I've ever seen in my life."

He was literally addressing his opening tee shot when an assistant in the pro shop next to the first tee came out and told him he had a phone call. "I said, 'It's kind of a bad time,'" recalls Lauer, who went in and picked up the phone to find Gumbel on the other end. "He was so excited about me playing Pebble for the first time. He had just gotten off the air in New York, ran to his office, and was, like, 'Now remember, on 9, keep the ball to the left. On 10 . . .' I go, 'Bryant, I'm just teeing off.' He goes, 'I'll only take a few minutes.' I said, 'You don't understand. *I'm just teeing off.* I'm standing over the ball!' He went through the entire back nine with me."

Carol Leifer

Stand-up comedienne Carol Leifer is the former *Seinfeld* writer credited with being the model for Julia Louis-Dreyfus's character, Elaine. She now stars in her own show on the WB, *Alright Already*. She's been playing golf for about two years, mostly at a par-3 course in the San Fernando Valley frequented by a lot of celebrities. She's not sure what her handicap is, because she doesn't always keep score.

"I'll get an 8 or 9 on certain holes," she says, "and I don't like to put down a 9. But I really, really love it. I feel like I'm learning stand-up comedy all over again. They're so similar. With stand-up, you have to really stink it up and be bad to get good. That's what so much of golf is about. You have to be bad to get good."

A sense of humor doesn't hurt either—both on stage and on the course. "There are a lot of holes I'd like to forget," says the comedienne. "The thing is, I choke a lot if I'm playing with strangers. About six weeks ago, George Clooney was in the foursome behind us at the par-3 course. It was really slow, so he was watching us most of the time we were teeing off. It was a little nerve-racking."

On this one 135-yard hole, it got so quiet as Leifer prepared to tee off with her 5-iron that you could almost hear the tee going into the ground. She proceeded to whiff the ball and do a 360. It looked more like an ice-skating move than a golf swing. Clooney looked at his partners and said, "I didn't see that. D'you see anything? Good practice swing." "So that kind of thing does throw me off," Leifer says, "but the day George Clooney can't throw me off is the day I'd worry about."

Jack Lemmon

When Jack Lemmon isn't acting on the set, he can usually be found at Hillcrest Country Club, located right across the street from 20th Century-Fox Studios, hitting golf balls. Truth be told, even when he's on the set he's often hitting golf balls. On the lot at Paramount in the late eighties while making *Dad* with Ted Danson, he had a net set up in an alley. "I was out there whacking balls all the time," says Lemmon, a 15-handicap who's broken 80 four or five times since he picked up the game at age thirty-five. "Golf is the greatest leveler there is. It's so damn difficult. Even though the ball doesn't move, you do, all too often."

Lemmon's travails trying to make the cut just once at the AT&T Pebble Beach National Pro-Am are legendary. For twenty-five years he's come up short. Of course, his chances aren't helped when he hits shots like the one he did some seventeen years ago when he scored a "hotel-in-one" off the first tee at Pebble. With spectators lining both sides of the fairway, Lemmon, who was staying in a first-floor room just to the right of the first fairway, took a mammoth swing and hit a screaming slice.

Jack Lemmon, AT&T Pebble Beach National Pro-Am, 1997

"Everyone on the right started yelling and ducking as the ball flew past them and toward the lodge," he recalls. "As I walked over there, I knew I had hit it near my room. Sure enough, there was Felicia, my wife, in her bathrobe, waving. She held up the ball and said, 'Good going.' The damn ball went right into my room. I'm not kidding. The sliding glass door was open and Felicia was in the john. The ball made so much noise bouncing around the room off the walls, she thought someone was firing a machine gun. It left marks all over the place, but, amazingly enough, it did not really break anything. When she came out, the ball was sitting in the middle of the carpet. I couldn't believe it, right into my room!"

Lemmon has suffered through a lot of bad holes in the thirty-five years he's been playing the game, but the worst came about twelve years ago at the AT&T. Playing the par-5 5th at Cypress Point Club, Lemmon hit his second shot into muddy area in the right rough. He tried to play an explosion shot, hitting an inch behind the ball.

"Well, I got the mud, then got the ball, and when the club wrapped around my neck the ball was still attached to it and went flying backward about forty yards," he recalls. "So now I'm forty yards farther away but at least it was back out in the fairway. I hit a 7-iron and landed in the trap beside the green. The trap is sopping wet, but I had to play the ball. It was in a wet but solid part of the sand. I had to stand half in a puddle. As I'm standing there addressing my shot, wiggling back and forth, I suddenly notice that the club is getting closer to my throat. I looked down and said, 'Christ, I'm sinking in the sand.' I took a quick slap at the thing. It went flying over the green into the other trap. Now, I'm totally disgusted and I'm out of the hole."

It got worse. He stuck his club out for his caddie to yank him out of the quagmire and nothing happened. His caddie pulled harder and Lemmon came flying out of his shoes and out of the trap. "Now I'm in my stocking feet, sopping wet, of course, and the shoes have disappeared totally," he says incredulously. "We weren't going to go back in there, so I finished the front nine and four more holes before I was close enough to the clubhouse to run up and get some kind of a pair of shoes. I played God-awful. I shot about 100 or something. The shoes are probably still in that trap."

Téa Leoni

*H*ow appropriate that Téa Leoni is one of the few female celebrities to play golf. The star of NBC's *Naked Truth*, Leoni is one tough dame in the mold of Katharine Hepburn. She's definitely in touch with her masculine side. Her idea of a great day is a macho round of golf followed by a cigar and a single-malt scotch. "When I'm on the golf course I feel like I'm playing hooky," says the lithe actress, who plays to about a 20-handicap. "It's a chunk of time where no one can find me. It's a real stress reducer, which is important in this business. As the saying goes, 'A bad day on the golf course is better than a good day in the office.'"

*H*er most memorable round came about two years ago on Maui's Plantation Course when she shot a "legitimate" 87 after she had been playing only nine months. "It's a really difficult course," she recalls. "It was one of those days where there was nothing missing from my bag. I was right on with my wedges, I was spot on with my putter. My drives were unbelievable, my 3-woods off the fairway were as smooth as silk. It was the best day I've ever had."

As always, she was playing with a bunch of guys. "I'm the only female of my set that plays, but I'm trying to get some of my gal

Téa Leoni, at home on the range

friends into it," says Leoni, who's savvy enough about the game to know not to watch someone with a bad swing for fear it'll rub off. "One of the guys I play with has got a horrible swing. It's so bad you can't pay attention to him. Every time he takes his backswing you're like this," she adds, covering her eyes, turning her head away, and grimacing.

Not all her golf experiences have been positive. She and her new husband, *The X-Files'* David Duchovny, were driving along the Pacific Coast Highway near Malibu when they got a flat. To change the tire, they had to unload everything from the trunk, including her brand-new set of Big Berthas.

"When we finished changing the tire, we forgot to put the clubs back in and we left them on PCH," Leoni laments. "At first I came crashing to my knees, but then I got a set of Tommy Armours with male shafts and I love them. I swing too quickly for a woman's club."

Then there was the time she broke her new Callaway putter on the 8th hole at Riviera while shooting the round of her life. "It had a new beveled hosel and the head just snapped off. It went flying, and I promise you there was no tree involved. I was just taking a practice stroke. I was left with no putter in my bag in what surely would have been one of my best rounds. I had to putt with a 2-iron. I don't think I broke 100."

Huey Lewis

Rocker Huey Lewis is such a big fan of the game that he called his 1986 album with his News bandmates *Fore!* He started playing three years before that while on his honeymoon in Kapalua, Hawaii. "Don't ask me why, but we brought my mother-in-law and sister-in-law along," he recalls. "All they wanted to do was go lay on the beach all day, so there was nothing for me to do. I rented some sticks and went up to the club, and I was hooked right away."

Lewis is now a 10-handicap who gets out two or three times a week at his home course, Meadow Club in Fairfax, California, north of San Francisco, which Alister MacKenzie designed right around the time he did Cypress Point Club. He recently had his best round ever at the course, a 2 over 73. He was playing with his usual group, which includes his drummer, Bill Gibson, and was 1 under through five holes. A double bogey on 9 left him 1 over on the front. He bogied 15 but got the stroke back on the next hole when he hit a 7-iron out of a hazard to within eight feet and sunk the birdie putt.

After a great drive on 17, a long par 4 and number-one handicap hole, Lewis left a 3-iron twenty-five feet from the pin. "I'm thinking to myself, 'Man, I'm 1 over par. I'm going to two-putt this thing and I'm going to have a putt on 18 for even par. This is amazing!' Then I say, 'Wait a minute, you idiot. You have this putt for even par! Let's make this thing.'"

And that's just what he does. "Bill Gibson looks at me and says, 'Wow, you're really playing well.' I look at him and I go, 'Even par!' Well, you know what happens next."

His tee ball on 18 was headed out-of-bounds but hit the only tree in the area and came careening back into the fairway, leaving him a 4-iron off a downslope. "I'm over it thinking, 'All I've got to do is get this on the friggin' green and I'm going to shoot even par. I know I'm never going to do this in my life—maybe once or twice.' All that's weighing on me. Well, I block it out, don't finish the swing. It ends up in some crap on the right. I hack it out of there into the bunker and I two-putt for double bogey. Mentally, you play best when you play shot to shot. As soon as you add them all up, you've given up already. You're already tallying. You're satisfied with what you've done."

Lewis has played in the AT&T Pebble Beach National Pro-Am for ten years. His biggest thrill came one year when he won the celebrity shoot-out with Joe Pesci in a chip-off. His worst moment, perhaps, came during his first AT&T when he nervously faced a 3-iron into 18 at Pebble with the gale-force wind in his face. "I blocked it right into the grandstand," he recalls. "And BAM! It hits some guy in the family jewels. I go over there and he wants me to autograph the ball, which I do. I take a drop, hit it into the bunker, where I lie 4. I almost hole the chip and make the putt for a 6. I later find out the guy wants to sue me for problems that he had that I guess were sexual, but I don't know. The tournament took care of it."

*T*he best piece of advice Lewis ever received came from his good friend Peter Jacobsen when they were playing a practice round together at the 1989 AT&T. "Jake's just chatting away like he does and having a ball," the singer recalls. "I'm playing poorly and I'm upset. I hit a bad shot and I throw my club down on the ground. Jake comes over to me with a concerned look on his face. He says, 'What the hell did you do that for?' I said, 'Because I'm pissed off.' He looked at me dead serious and says, 'You're not good enough to be pissed off.' I've always tried to remember that."

Hal Linden

*T*he *Barney Miller* star has a dilemma: he's playing better than ever but is not scoring any better. "I'm hitting the ball great off the tee but now I'm far enough to get into trouble," Hal Linden laments. "The shot that's killing me is the approach shot. I just can't put it on. I'm always in some kind of trouble near the green and I end up with bogey, double-bogey, at a time I shouldn't. I'll be sixty yards from the green in two on a par 5 and I'll end up with a 7 because I'll hit the ball over into a trap or something. I just don't have that touch to put it tight."

Linden, an 18-handicap who plays three times a week, belongs to Brentwood Country Club in Los Angeles, which he joined when he moved out from New York in the seventies to do *Barney Miller*. "It's very difficult to be a golfer living in New York," he says. "There's no golf in The Bronx. Fageddaboutit."

*O*ne of his most memorable golfing moments came when he was playing in the pro-am at the Legends of Golf tournament at PGA West five years ago. Playing the back side of the Nicklaus Resort Course first, his group came to their final hole, the number-one handicap 9th hole, tied for the lead. Linden was a 19-handicap so he got two strokes on the long par-4 hole with a lake fronting the green. After hitting a decent drive, Linden thought about laying up but decided to go for it with a 7-iron. Since they were one of the last groups, everyone else was already in, gathered around the green awaiting his shot. His anxiety got the better of him, however; he caught the ball fat and it appeared to go into the lake.

As he walked up the fairway, he muttered to himself, "You blew it, you blew your two-stroke hole. Why didn't you lay up, chip on, take your two putts, we'd pick up a stroke." He was about to drop a ball when he noticed that the lake wasn't quite full. Much to his delight, his ball came to rest in a muddy area at water's edge. "I've never hit out of mud in my life," Linden recalls. "I grabbed the A player and he told me basically to hit a flop shop. Shoes and all I slogged into the mud. Everybody's watching. I just said, 'Here goes nothing.' I took a swat, got a face full of mud, but the ball popped up onto the green. I two-putted for the 5 net 3, and we won the tournament by one stroke. And let me tell you something, everybody else was either wet or in sand. It was me out of the four guys."

Linden took the win in stride, having won his share of celebrity tournaments. "I've got a lot of plaques. Plaques I got. Would you like some plaques?"

Robert Loggia

The raspy-voiced actor, who has had leading roles in such films as *Independence Day* and *Big*, is a natural athlete who took to the game confidently when he started in 1990, parring the first hole he ever played. "I said, 'Oh, for God's sake, what is this dumb game? It's just so damn easy,'" he recalls. "Then, of course, the roof fell in. I never parred another hole after that. It's brought me to my knees. I thought my athletic skills would segue into golf, but somebody gave me thoughts on what the swing is, and that was it."

A former A-level tennis player, Loggia was a bit forced into taking up the game. His doctor told him he was looking at a hip replacement if he kept pounding it in tennis. "What the hell am I going to do?" he asked the doctor, who replied, "Take up golf." "I became addicted right away," says Loggia, who joined Bel-Air and broke 100 right away. "But breaking 90 is like a brick wall."

Now an 18-handicap, Loggia loves the character-revealing aspects of the game. "There are cheap shots in other sports," he says. "But golf is a game of honor. You have to keep your composure, you can't play out of heat, as you can in other sports. It has cost me friendships, I must say, because when I played golf with some guys who are dishonest, I lose respect for them and I won't play with them again. The way someone plays golf, the way they win or lose, is the most incredibly true reflection of the person's inner character."

*I*n 1992, Loggia played in the AT&T Pebble Beach National Pro-Am for the first and last time. "It is unbelievable," he says. "The gallery doesn't "V" out—they "V" in. People line the fairway three deep from tee to green. It's like Times Square. Imagine, here I am, a 24-handicap, trying to hit the ball down the middle. The people are trusting that I'm not going to hit them. Indeed, I hit a girl at Poppy Hills. Thank God she had a baseball cap on. She ducked her head, but the ball still struck her in the forehead, right at the hairline, and left a gash. One of the members of our foursome said, 'Oh, c'mon, people get hit out here all the time.' I said, 'Bullshit.' I threw my clubs down. I was really upset."

Loggia had duck-hooked his drive during a practice round, striking the young woman about eighty yards from the tee. "I thought it had hit a tree when I heard the sound," recalls the actor, who rushed to her aid. "I picked her up and took her in my car to the infirmary, where they stitched her up. She wore it as a badge of merit almost. She was proud of it, that she had gotten brained at the AT&T by Robert Loggia, but it caused me incredible trauma. I'll never play in another one, I'll tell you that."

Rob Lowe

*I*t's safe to say that former Brat Packer Rob Lowe is the only celebrity ever to eagle a hole in Luxembourg. Heck, he's probably the only celebrity to ever play golf there. He was shooting a movie for Showtime there a few years back and playing golf at the tiny European country's only country club. He was shocked by some of the handicap postings. "I've never seen anybody claiming a 40-handicap but they were," he says. "That tells you about the state of golf in Luxembourg. You know what? If I did have a handicap that high I sure as hell wouldn't post it. But it was the best golf game I ever had. The conditions were sort of chilly. When it's blistering heat I wilt. The leaves were turning. It was just that time you want to be out on a golf course."

His eagle came on the 18th hole, a dog-leg left par 5. "What I shot in the round has faded from my memory," remembers the actor, who plays to a 16-handicap. "But I was playing with a new driver and decided to cut off the hole. Got it. I had a hideous, hanging lie. I hit a 5-wood from there to about four feet from the pin. I'm in the cart driving to the green going, 'Okay, this is it. You've got a shot for the eagle here.' I sank it before I had the chance to think too much about it. Eagles are hard to come by. There was no miracle shot, which was really nice. It wasn't like I knocked in a forty-five-foot putt. Three good shots on any given day is cause for celebration."

*L*owe, who's surprisingly articulate and passionate about the game, grew up in Ohio, where he learned the game from his grandfather, Bob Hepler, a restaurateur and community pillar who built the Shelby County Golf Club in 1968. "I'd go there on the weekends with him all the time," Lowe says. "I liked to look for the frogs in the ponds. It was only as I got older that I got more interested in the game. I love the natural beauty of it, the way the light hits the fairway, the way the grass smells. It reminds me of those times when I was young and really carefree and being out with my grandfather, who I loved dearly. Mostly I love the discipline of it and the concentration it takes. It's a concentration that I really lack for the most part in my own life. And as my interests expand in business, I have an opportunity to do a lot of business on a golf course. And if you don't know what a guy's about after a round of golf, you haven't been watching."

Amazingly, his grandfather has recorded eleven holes in one! Rob's had zero, but he came close one time, oh so close, when he just started playing seriously five or six years ago. He was shooting the Stephen King miniseries *The Stand* in Utah and got to play Salt Lake City Country Club one day with the pro. Just as Lowe was about to hit his 3-wood on a downhill 206-yard par 3, the pro said, "Look at your ball"—he was about an inch over the line. "I'd hate for you to have a hole in one and not be able to count it." Lowe gave him a smirk, re-teed his ball, and proceeded to fire a missile right at the hole. The ball hit once, bounced, and stuck on the lip of the cup "like it was nailed there," he says. "The ball was actually protruding over the cup. I tried the shadow trick, but it didn't work."

The what? "The shadow trick. If the ball is over the cup in the direct sunlight, if you put your hand over the ball and shadow the ball, in theory the ball will contract due to lack of heat and it might start to roll. I tried jumping up and down. The pro could not believe it. Literally half the ball was over the hole. You couldn't place it any better. He was just devastated. He said, 'I want to report this as an ace so badly.' I said, 'I know. Me too.'"

*L*ike anyone with a family (he has two young boys), Lowe doesn't play nearly as much golf as he'd like. "Golf is very much of a binge sport for me," he says. "I'll go through a period where I'll play twice a week pretty consistently for five, six months, depending on how busy the home life is. Then I'll go through periods where I won't play for months."

He lives in the Santa Barbara, California, area, and doesn't belong to a club, so he plays many of the great public courses there, like Sandpiper, where he had his best round ever, an 83 from the tips. "What I remember about that round is it's sort of like being in a thicket of trees when you're a player who shoots in the high 80s and 90s, and every once in a while you get a glimpse out of the thicket to what it's like in the beautiful green meadow," he says. "Then, of course, you get lost in the thicket again. I was sort of getting a glimpse. My second shot is the gremlin of my game. I feel great on the tee, but as the second shot goes, so goes my round."

Lee Majors

"T he Six Million Dollar Man," Lee Majors, is a golfaholic who plays just about every day at one of the several courses to which he belongs in the Fort Lauderdale, Florida, area. His favorite is Adios Country Club, a men-only course where he plays to a 12-handicap, a number he's pretty much been at since he started playing thirty years ago. "Never got any better, never got any worse," says Majors, who's hampered by a bad left knee, an old football injury aggravated by years of doing stunts. "I can't make too good of a turn through the ball, so I use a lot more woods now. I still have pretty good arm power, being bionic, you know."

Superhero strength isn't always a blessing. Playing the Dinah Shore tournament in Rancho Mirage, California, in the seventies, Majors was introduced with his superhuman moniker. "The gallery expected a huge drive," he recalls. "I think I hit it about four or five feet. I dribbled it off the tee. I topped it. It wasn't really a bionic hit. Total embarrassment. I told them I was a quart low. I hit it from there and got the heck out of there."

One year in the seventies at Jackie Gleason's tournament at Inverrary Country Club in Fort Lauderdale, Majors was partnered in the pro-am with his hero, Arnold Palmer. On one hole Arnie promised Majors he was going to hit a 7-iron to within five feet of the pin. Waiting for the green to clear, the newly bespectacled Palmer went over to the gallery. "He came back over, took his 7-iron out and he hit the ball clean over the green," Majors recalls. "As we were walking up, I said, 'I thought you were going to hit it within five feet of the pin.' And he said, 'Lee, these glasses are going to be the end of me. When I looked over to the gallery, I saw this girl. She had on a tank top. It looked like two fried eggs. So, on my backswing, that's what I was thinking of, and I think the adrenaline got going.'"

One of his regular partners at Adios is Wendy's founder Dave Thomas. They play quickly, usually in about three hours. "I never take a practice swing," says Majors, who's broken 80 a few times. "We just hit and go."

Last year, he had a hole in one, but unfortunately he wasn't playing with Thomas when he knocked it in from 160 yards with a 6-iron. The two, along with another partner, have a bet that if anybody gets a hole in one the other two have to pay $5,000. "I called them up and said, 'Do you have to be there?'" Majors says. "They said, 'Yes.' But Dave got a hole in one on the same hole a couple years ago, and we didn't pay him because we weren't with him, either."

Joe Mantegna

Best known for his lead roles in such films as *The Godfather: Part III* and *Bugsy*, Joe Mantegna is a 20-handicap who takes a lighthearted approach to the game. "I'm not a very competitive person," he says. "I really like to go out, smoke a cigar, walk around, and have some fun with whomever I'm playing. I'm approaching fifty now, so it's too late for me to take it seriously. But what I love about the game is the integrity of it, the honor of it when it's played right, the history of it and the self-policing of it, the dignity of it."

Mantegna learned to play the game from his father, Joe Sr., an insurance salesman, while growing up in Chicago. "My dad really loved it. He tried to golf every day. And golfing in Chicago isn't the easiest thing in the world, either," says Mantegna, who was in a band in the sixties, arriving home from many gigs at five in the morning. "I'd be walking in the door with a guitar case and my dad would be walking out carrying golf clubs. We'd pass each other on the stairs. 'See ya, Dad.' 'Yeah, see ya, son.'"

His dad passed away when Joe was twenty-one, and Joe lost interest in the game. Then, five years ago, he was invited to play in Frank Sinatra's celebrity tournament in Palm Springs. "I thought,

'Oh my God, I can't pass this up to go meet Sinatra,'" he says. "I borrowed a pair of shoes from one friend and a set of clubs from another. I went to the driving range and whacked a few so I wouldn't totally embarrass myself, and I wound up winning it! I come in there not having played in fifteen years, and the next thing I know I'm standing between Frank Sinatra and Tony Bennett, who was the entertainer that year. They were thrusting microphones in my face, saying, 'How do you feel?' 'I feel like I'm in Italian heaven—what, are you kidding?'"

After his victory, pictures of him and Sinatra appeared in golf publications and he started getting calls to play. He also got a free set of clubs from the Tommy Armour company. "Turns out the head of their public relations department is a girl I went to high school with," Mantegna says. "She said, 'Joe, what kind of clubs do you use?' I said, 'Honey, I'm using a borrowed set from a friend of mine.' She said, 'Oh, we'll give you a set.' So now I'm a staff member. It's me and Jim Gallagher."

*L*ike most actors, Mantegna tends to play better with an audience around, which was the case last year while making the TV miniseries *The Last Don*. After filming some golf scenes at the Marriott Hotel in Palm Desert, California, Mantegna and his costars—Jason Gedrick, Seymour Cassel, and Cliff De Young—kept on playing after slipping the starter a few bucks.

"Cliff was playing pretty well," says Mantegna, who wasn't. "And he's one of these guys that, when he's playing well, he's letting everybody know it. He's getting on our nerves a little bit. We get up to the 17th hole and the entire film crew is on that tee box. I said, 'Boys, is the camera ready? Start rolling. You're going to get a fuckin' shot

they're gonna use on *Wide World of Sports*.' I'll be cocky like that, fig-
uring if I duff everyone will get a laugh. Well, I get up and I cream
one. It was my best drive of the day. Cliff does not play well under
pressure, and I'm saying, 'C'mon, Cliff, let's see what you can do.' He
hooks it, hits his worst shot of the day. Then, of course, I turn to the
camera and say, 'He's been doing that all day. We've been carrying
the guy.'"

Cheech Marin

Cheech Marin is new to the game, having just picked it up a couple of years ago when he won the role of Kevin Costner's sidekick and caddie in *Tin Cup*. Now he's a 20-handicap who's already broken 90 a few times. "I've finally learned how to hit my irons, how to hit down on them," says Marin, who picked up a lot of pointers from all the tour pros who made cameos in *Tin Cup*. "Just watching those guys do their magic was amazing."

One example of that came during a break in filming at La Paloma Country Club in Tucson, Arizona, where most of the movie was shot. Phil Mickelson put on a little clinic for fellow pros Craig Stadler, Fred Couples, and Corey Pavin, as well as Marin, Costner, costar Don Johnson, and director Ron Shelton. "We're standing below this big, tall pine tree that must have been eighty feet tall," Marin recalls. "Mickelson was taking $20 bets that he could stand an arm's length away from the tree and hit a ball over the tree with a sand wedge. Everybody put their money up, and zooooom! it went straight up and landed on the other side of the tree. Then he bet 'em that he could do it with a 9-iron, and he did it again. I couldn't believe it. He collected all the money and walked off."

Dean Martin

*T*he only thing Dean Martin liked to do more than drink was play golf. How often did he play? "How many days in the week are there?" asks his former agent, Mort Viner. "He loved being outdoors, hitting golf balls and being with the guys." Martin filmed his long-running NBC variety show only one day a week, but he played even on that day. "He'd still get in eighteen before work, because he didn't have to be at the studio till noon," Viner adds. "About the only time he didn't play was when he was making a movie and had to be on the set early."

Martin, who hosted the PGA Tour's Tucson tournament in the seventies, played to a 6-handicap at Bel-Air Country Club, where he almost won the club championship in the mid-sixties. "He shot a 69 in the finals and got beat by a guy who shot a 68," Viner says. Martin left the club for Riviera Country Club in 1967 when Bel-Air redid their greens. But wherever he played, he always liked to bet big with a whole group of golfers.

"They'd have four carts full of golfers. Bets would be going back and forth," says *Los Angeles Times* sports columnist and Riviera member Jim Murray, recalling a time he and Sid James, then managing editor of *Sports Illustrated*, were playing behind Martin. "On the 18th hole Dean hit a perfectly acceptable drive, but it went a little right and he flung his driver in anger. Sid said, 'Good Lord, he doesn't get

Dean Martin, always the swinger, on the Los Angeles set of *Some Came Running*, 1958

any fun out of the game. If we hit a drive like that we'd give a party.'
I said, 'Well, Sid, it probably cost him $2,000.'"

*T*hough Dean Martin passed away a few years ago, you can still see his smooth swing in the 1953 film he made with Jerry Lewis, *The Caddy*. You also get to hear him sing his signature song, "That's Amore." Would that the rest of the film lived up to Martin's on-course and crooning abilities. Lewis plays the title character to Martin's pro. Their fairway antics get them banned from the pro tour, but not before teeing it up with the likes of Ben Hogan, Sam Snead, and Byron Nelson.

Dick Martin

*T*he former cohost of *Laugh-In*, Dick Martin picked up the game some forty years ago, getting down to a 9-handicap at one point. Now a 17, Martin plays about three times a week at Bel-Air Country Club. When he first started, and he and his partner, Dan Rowan, were on the road, golf was their salvation. They played all day long, then did two shows at night. Indeed, the courses they got to play oftentimes dictated what venues they would book. Houston, Pittsburgh, and Akron, Ohio, were three of their favorite stops, since they got to play with Jackie Burke and Jimmy Demaret at Champions Golf Club, Lew Worsham at Oakmont Country Club, and Bobby Nichols at Firestone Country Club, respectively. "Going around playing these great courses was one of my biggest kicks," Martin says. "It was like a dreamworld, like we were on a pro tour."

Rowan quit playing in the early seventies out of frustration, even though he was about a 12-handicap. "He was very impatient," Martin says. "He was kind of a club-thrower. He expected more out of the game than I did. So he took up tennis and became quite a good player. I remember when Johnny Carson quit golf because he was very much the same temperament and, oddly enough, took up tennis, too. I went on alone on the Carson show one night and we got talking about golf, and he said, 'Well, I understand Dan quit.' I said, 'Yes, he's taking up sailing, because I figure how far can he throw a boat?'"

*I*n the late fifties, Martin and Rowan were in London performing at the Palladium when they got a call from Bob Hope, who was in France making *Paris Holiday* and invited them over to play. "I don't even remember the name of the course, but we were with Charles Lanvin of Lanvin perfume and some duke," Martin recalls. "We're on about the fifth hole and Hope says, 'This is for the usual four thousand, isn't it?' And I started to shit 'cause I didn't have any money. Well, it turned out to be francs. A dollar forty. Who knew?"

*M*artin was one of a handful of stars to play in a sort of celebrity Ryder Cup held at Gleneagles Hotel in Scotland in 1975–76. The American stars received two first-class tickets and a complimentary stay at the luxurious hotel just for playing one match against the British stars. An edited version was then shown on the BBC. Martin couldn't believe his good fortune. "When I got to the hotel," he recalls, "I said to the guy, 'I don't like to take advantage of anyone, but when you say complimentary everything, do you mean any kind of beverage?' 'Yes, sir.' 'How 'bout wine?' 'Any wine in the house.' I sent for that wine list so fast. I was getting 1961 La Tours and La Fites."

Each side also had a pro as captain and playing partner. The first year the Americans had Tom Weiskopf, while the British had Peter Oosterhuis. But it's the second year that Martin remembers most. "It was Sean Connery's gang against Bing Crosby's gang. It was really something. We had George C. Scott and Alan Shepard. They had Jackie Stewart. We had Johnny Miller, they had Tony Jacklin. It was like a pro tournament. The caddie wore a bib with your name on the back and someone carried one of those placards indicating how many over or under you were. You weren't allowed carts—or buggies, as they called them. But Bing got a buggy so he could go around and check on his team. He came by once, and I'm about eight feet off the green. I took the putter out, and it must have been about forty feet over swales and humps. Bing said, 'How you guys doing?' I said, 'Great,' and I sunk the forty-footer. 'Well, I guess so,' Bing said. Oh, God, we had fun."

Harpo Marx

Although Harpo Marx was always the silent one on-screen, he was a scream on the golf course. A member at Hillcrest Country Club, Harpo had a perpetual 20-handicap despite nearly daily play. He had what was perhaps the first oversize driver, but he didn't use it to shave strokes off his game; he used it for sustenance. The club usually held a sandwich under its hinged lid. Whenever a crowd gathered, Harpo would pull out the sandwich, take a bite, then put it back in.

Hillcrest had a rule that allowed golfers to remove their shirts after the 1st hole as long as they put them back on before playing the 9th. Eric Monti, who was Hillcrest's head pro for forty-seven years, recalls one of Harpo's antics. "One day when he was playing badly, he came up to the 9th and put his shirt on but took his pants off and played in his undershorts. There was no rule against that."

Harpo didn't care much for rules. Sam Snead was playing with the comedian when he motioned to "bump" his ball from just off the green. "He didn't like his lie," Snead remembers, "but I said, 'No, no, there's nothing wrong with that. The lie is real good.' But then he did that thing where he took both hands to form a woman to make me look away. When I turned around, his ball was in ground under repair. I said, 'All right, you've got to drop it over your shoulder.' He turned his back to the hole and threw right over his shoulder onto the green. Now he's got about a six-footer. He motioned, 'Good, good, in the leather?' He never said anything. I said, 'No, that's not in the leather.' He put the end of the putter in the hole and stretched it out to about six and a half feet. I said, 'Well, okay.' He just looked at me with that silly grin he had."

Tim Matheson

*T*hough he's mostly in TV movies these days, Tim Matheson is probably best known for his 1978 feature role as Otter in *National Lampoon's Animal House*, which contains the best golf lesson ever given in a movie. He and costar Peter Riegert take aim at an ROTC officer on horseback who's mistreating one of their fraternity-house pledges. After Riegert misses, Matheson advises, "Your left arm is straight, but you're not keeping your head down. Always try to hit through the ball." With that, he nails the horse in the rump and the officer is dragged off screaming.

In reality, it was Matheson, a golfing novice then, who needed the lesson that day when they shot the scene at the University of Oregon. Before shooting the scene, Matheson thought he'd get in a little practice but came down with the golfing equivalent of stage fright. "I couldn't hit a ball to save my life," he recalls. "Of course, every golfer on the crew stopped by to help. It was one of those panic moments. By the time we're ready to shoot, I'm so screwed up. I had to do four or five takes because I wasn't making solid contact. It's one of the worst golf swings ever recorded on film, although people have graciously ignored that. The scene is so funny, I guess it really doesn't matter how bad the swing is. I'm supposed to know what I'm doing, and I look like hell. That's acting and special effects."

*N*ow about a 16-handicap, Matheson lives near Santa Barbara, where he plays many of the fine public courses in the area with other actors like Jay Thomas and Bruce McGill, who played D-Day in *Animal House* and made a sojourn to Scotland with Matheson in September 1983. At the time, McGill was costarring on Broadway in *My One and Only* with Tommy Tune and Twiggy. Matheson, who had free airline tickets to Scotland, wanted him to quit the play to go on the trip, but McGill was reluctant. "It's a matter of form," he tried to explain. "You can't leave before the stars." In true *Animal House* "road trip" fashion, Matheson responded, "Screw them! It's golf—in Scotland, for God's sake!"

Nothing further needed to be said. McGill quit the show and insisted on taking care of all the arrangements for hotels and start times. "I know a guy who's really connected," he said. Famous last words. They had absolutely no reservations for anything, as they soon found out after landing in Edinburgh.

"We get to the rental car place and they've never heard of us," Matheson recalls. "But we just said, 'Fuck it, we're here, how bad can it be?' I'm telling you, it was the absolute, most magical best trip I've ever taken in my life. Everything fell into place like you wouldn't believe. The rental-car guy gives us the best deal you've ever gotten on a car. We drove straight to St. Andrews, where there's a special little bed-and-breakfast place called the Old Course Hotel right on the Firth of Fourth. They don't have any reservations, of course. They say we can stay one night overlooking the Firth, but after that it's pretty questionable. They liked us, because we were silly and having a good time. We weren't like the ugly Americans. We were just, 'Whatever. Anything you can do is fine. We're going to play golf.'"

They ended up staying in the room a whole week and playing the Old Course just about every morning at the break of dawn. After lunch or a nap, they'd get in another eighteen at Carnoustie or Gullen. "One day we got back around four-thirty and there's nobody on the tee at the Old Course, which is right in the heart of town," Matheson says. "I looked at Bruce and he said, 'Ah, I want to go take a nap.' I said, 'Yeah, right, we've got the tee at the Old Course. We're in Scotland and *you*, you don't want to play golf. Drop me off here.' Sure enough, he joins me. We played fifty-four holes that day."

After St. Andrews they drove to Gleneagles and played all three courses there for three days, followed by a few more days at Royal Dornoch. "Again, everything would fall into place," Matheson says. "The people were so great. It got to be so ludicrous, because every need we had was fulfilled."

The final payoff came as they tried to catch their flight out of Scotland back to London. When they got to the small airport, they discovered that the arrival of Princess Anne had canceled all flights in and out. "We thought, 'Now we're fucked,'" Matheson recalls. "We had to drive to the next airport fifty miles away, so we raced down there. We were supposed to leave the rental car at some gas station ten miles away, but we don't have time. As we pull into the airport, a uniformed matron from the rental-car company is standing right in front of the airport. I just leaned out the window and said, 'Can we check this car in with you?' She said, 'Oh, lads, I would be so happy to take it for you.' I said, 'Great!' because we had about three minutes to catch this plane. We ran and jumped on the plane. It all worked out perfectly."

Meatloaf

*C*orpulent rock star Meatloaf has been playing seriously for only a year, but already he's broken 100. A member of the tony Sherwood Country Club north of Los Angeles, Meatloaf plays to a 27-handicap. He calls the game "a great friendship vehicle. It's a great way to get people together. I'm terrible with dinner. I fall asleep and want to lay on the floor. I'm like a five-year-old in a restaurant. Golf is great, because I'm not confined. I get real antsy at dinner, especially if they go more than an hour. I like that drive-through stuff."

When he and his friends get together at Sherwood, cigars are welcome and cell phones are banned. One of the people Meatloaf likes to tee it up with is tour pro Steve Pate. One day they were playing with two other friends when the singer somehow managed to get the ball behind him on eight tee shots. "I kid you not," Meatloaf says. "I hit trees, it went backwards. I hit rocks, it went backwards. I hit the golf cart and it went backwards. There was one hole where, I swear, the ball ended up fifty or sixty yards behind us. I hit the ball really well, but it hit a rock in front of the tee and came straight back, way high in the air right over our heads. It went over the black tees and into the bushes. Steve was rolling around on the ground, laughing. He told me after that it was the best round of golf he had every played. He had more fun with me than in all his time of playing golf."

*I*n his first tournament, Meatloaf finished second in the "horse race" and won $260 playing with one of his managers, another 27-handicapper. "On the first hole there's about forty guys standing there looking at me," he recalls. "I hit the second-longest drive. They were going, 'Whoa! You're good in front of an audience.' All I need is a gallery. The concentration's up. I'm performing. I should be like Michael Jackson, hire a hundred people to follow me around."

Bill Murray

*D*ue, no doubt, to his zany role as Carl the greenskeeper in 1980's *Caddyshack* and his hilarious antics at the AT&T Pebble Beach National Pro-Am, Bill Murray has become the alpha and omega of celebrity golf. There is no one fans would rather watch more, so entertaining is he on the course. Scott Simpson has played with the comedian at the AT&T Pebble Beach National Pro-Am since 1993. "He played one year before and there were some articles about whether he should be invited back or not, whether he was distracting," says the pro. "Peter Jacobsen said, 'You guys'd be great together.' So I wrote the tournament and said, 'I'd love to play with him, and he wouldn't bother me. We'd have a lot of fun.' And we have. I've seen it where he'll slice the ball into a part of the gallery and everyone in that area will start cheering because they know he's going to be over there in a few minutes. I've never seen anything like that before."

Only Murray could have people cheering a slice. With Murray, golf loses any pretensions it might have. Even the normally staid group photo becomes wacky, like the time they did a pyramid with the caddies. Many of his hijinks are of the you-had-to-be-there variety, but one year at Poppy Hills, Murray's old canvas bag was lined up on the first tee with all the shiny new tour bags. When one of the marshals asked, "Hey, Bill, where's your old bag?" he walked over to

Bill Murray, Hard Rock Cafe Celebrity/Charity Golf Tournament, Thousand Oaks, California, 1997

the gallery, put his arm around an elderly woman, and said, "Here's my old bag, right here."

It was his fondness for old ladies, though, that almost caused Murray to get banned from the AT&T after his and Simpson's first year together. Coming up the 18th fairway followed by two fans dressed in camouflage fatigues and branch-covered helmets (à la *Caddyshack*), Murray turned to Simpson and said, "You know, this has been so much fun, we've just got to do something on the last hole."

Recalls Simpson: "He has a real soft spot in his heart for older people. He always goes out of his way to try and make them feel special. Here was this little old lady in a tweed skirt who's actually been watching the tournament for forty years. She looked like she was right from Scotland. He brought her out and danced around in the bunker. He let go of her and she fell, then he fell down and started doing snow angels. It was so funny. Everyone was cracking up."

Everyone, that is, except for then–PGA Tour commissioner Deane Beman and traditionalists like Tom Watson. "I heard all kinds of excuses, like it's bad to give the gallery the feeling they can come out and bother the players," Simpson says. "I think Watson said something like 'Well, I'm not sure we're going to get that bunker raked. Bill's like, 'Hey, I grew up being a caddie. You don't think I'm going to rake the bunker. C'mon.'"

On the night before the next year's event, Beman sent a message to Murray via tournament chairman Lou Russo to cool it. "The Bill Murray thing," he said, "is inappropriate, detrimental, and will not be tolerated in the future." He went on to say that Murray's antics crossed the line of entertainment and were creating a "circus" atmosphere.

After Murray half-jokingly called for Beman's resignation and said he was creating "a Nazi state," he was isolated from the other celebrity pairings and from getting any TV time. "Beman actually had Tour officials follow us around, making sure he didn't do anything that was out-of-bounds," Simpson says. "It kind of made it miserable for us. Bill said, 'Fine, if that's the way they want it, then this is my last AT&T.'" By the time they got to the 18th green, the CBS cameras were long covered up. "You guys?" Murray yelled up at the empty tower. "This is my big putt on 18. Are you getting it? Is anybody left at CBS?" The gallery ate it up. "They lost football. Did they lose golf, too?" More laughter.

After tapping in his final putt, Murray pulled a baseball bat from his bag and had one of his playing partners, Chicago Cubs first baseman Mark Grace, pitch him a golf ball, which he launched into the Pacific. Then he turned into Carlton Fisk in the '75 World Series, jumping and motioning with his arms for the ball to stay fair. The crowd roared as he broke into a home-run trot around the green and said, "My last shot at the AT&T until Beman resigns."

Fortunately for most fans of golf, Beman resigned later that year and Murray was back in full view and form at the '95 AT&T.

*H*igh jinks aside, Murray loves to play and has a deep appreciation for the game. He has a terrific swing that looks better than his 15-handicap. "He just doesn't practice a whole lot," Simpson says. "He's real off-and-on. His whole game is inconsistent. He'd be a great scramble or best ball partner. He'll have a lot of good holes and then he'll mess up some holes."

Their best year at the AT&T came in 1996 when they made the cut. "He was really excited," Simpson recalls. "First of all, you don't have to hear about Jack Lemmon anymore, so that's pretty good. We had a great party that night. He was sampling some wines. We were

Bill Murray, Alice Cooper, Jack Wagner, and Jack Nicholson, Hard Rock Cafe
Celebrity/Charity Golf Tournament, Thousand Oaks, California, 1997

up till about one and we had to tee off about eight A.M. We started
on the 10th hole. He hit a driver and a 3-iron in there about five feet.
He got over the putt and said, 'Oh my God, I don't know if I can
hit this thing.' That wine was still bothering him a little bit. He
missed it but still made a par net birdie. He actually played pretty
good that day, but just getting started that early was a little tough."

*M*urray has always wanted to caddie for Simpson. He finally
got his chance at the '97 Motorola Western Open outside
Chicago, Murray's hometown, when Simpson's regular caddie, Mike
Dunsmore, had to go to a wedding. "He didn't need any pointers. He
caddied a lot when he was a kid growing up in Chicago, so he knows

the game of golf really well," says Simpson, who figured out the yardages with Murray. "But I don't rely on my caddie to tell me what club to hit or to read the greens, so he was off the hook in that regard."

On the seventy-first hole, Simpson hit a bunker shot to within two feet of the hole, which Bill promptly took credit for in front of the huge gallery. "After I made par, I said, 'Well, if you're taking all the credit, I might as well get the bag,'" says Simpson, who carried the bag to the 18th tee while Murray pretended to be the tour player. "It was a lot of fun. It's no problem having him out there. Some of the other players we played with played really well," including Simpson himself, who was one of the leaders after shooting 67 in the second round.

Simpson even saved himself $600 and 5 percent of his winnings (a typical caddie's salary). "How do you pay a guy who makes $10 million a picture?" he asks. "But I'll pay him in some way, there's no doubt about that. We'll work something out."

Graham Nash

Rock star Graham Nash had been playing the game for only two months when he accomplished something few who play their whole life ever do: he had a hole in one. In October 1981, he was with three friends at the Princeville Golf Club on Kauai when they came to a 186-yard par 3. "I had no idea what I was doing," he recalls. "I never trusted my woods, because no beginning golfer does, so I hit a 1-iron off the tee. I didn't know I wasn't supposed to hit a 1-iron either."

He teed up his orange ball and made a smooth pass at it. When he saw that the ball was headed toward the green, he stooped down to pick up his tee. "When I looked up, I couldn't see my ball and I thought, 'Well, shit, it's gone over the hole.' The other guys weren't paying attention, either. We drove around and everybody's got their ball. Mine's the only ball nowhere to be seen. We walked on the green and there it is in the hole. I just went, 'Wow!' I thought, 'Fuck, this is a great game.' Don't tell me it didn't piss off the professional at the club who had been playing for forty years and never got close. The Zen of it, hitting a one-inch ball into a four-inch cup from 186 yards in one shot, it staggered me. I've been trying to get back there ever since."

*N*ash is a 17-handicap who belongs to Braemar Country Club in Los Angeles. He gets out only twice a month and wishes it were more. "I like a lot of things about the game," he says. "But my primary love is that it is so graceful. The *lowest* score wins. It's completely anti-American. There is no body contact. You are on your honor and you are only really playing against the course. And you're playing against yourself, because it takes a great deal of honor and discipline not to kick your ball out from under a tree or say you took a four when you really took an eighteen."

Nash, who's a member of the Shivas Irons Society, plays often with John Ashworth, of the golf clothing company, and fellow Crosby, Stills, and Nash member Stephen Stills, who's a 22-handicap. "His game is . . . let me see, *volatile* is a good word," Nash says. "When he is on, he can drive great and he has a fabulous flop shot, but he's very erratic. He gets a little angry sometimes. I've seen his anger defeat his game."

*H*is most memorable round came a few years ago on the island of Bali in Indonesia at the Bali Handara golf club. It wasn't his score (a 94) that made it such an unforgettable experience, though; it was the setting. Recalls Nash: "I have a friend who's a golf pro there, and he says, 'I'll pick you up at four.' I said, 'Are we going to be able to play eighteen?' He said, 'No, no, four in the morning. It's two hours to get there, and we want to go off at dawn.' Dig this: up four and a half thousand feet into a fucking volcano, over the rim into the actual volcano where there's an eighteen-hole golf course of doom. It's unbelievable. Once you get down into the rim you can't see anything apart from 360 degrees of trees. It's beautiful, it's like heaven."

Jack Nicholson, Police-Celebrity Golf Tournament, Los Angeles, 1997

Jack Nicholson

When Jack Nicholson isn't hiding behind his sunglasses at a Lakers game, he can usually be found on the golf course. He loves to play, even though he struggles with the game and rarely counts all his strokes. "He hits two-putts and then picks up," says one Bel-Air Country Club member. "You don't bet him for money."

Though his handicap is purportedly a 10, he looks more like a 20. He has a hard, low follow-through that looks a little like he's furiously turning a steering wheel to the left to avoid a car accident—which is appropriate, given that the most famous golf story about Jack Nicholson didn't take place on the golf course but on a city street. That would be the time, of course, he attacked a fellow Los Angeles driver in February 1994.

Salesman Robert Blank had stopped at a light in Toluca Lake, not far from Lakeside Golf Club, one of the three L.A. clubs to which Nicholson belongs. A late-model black Mercedes pulled up alongside Blank's 1969 Mercedes and two men emerged from the car, one of whom was an enraged Nicholson. "You cut me off," he shouted before repeatedly striking the roof of Blank's car with a 3-iron. Nicholson then attacked the front windshield, the shattered glass causing minor cuts to Blank's nose.

The city's attorney's office filed misdemeanor assault and vandalism charges against the actor, while Blank slapped him with a civil suit. The suit was settled out of court a few months later, however, when Blank accepted a reported settlement of $500,000, which also resulted in the judge's dropping the criminal counts. The cause of Nicholson's rage wasn't a bad round that morning, but rather a difficult shooting schedule on the film he was making, *The Crossing Guard*, as well as the recent death of one of his closest friends.

*T*he club Nicholson used in the attack was most likely a Callaway, since that's all he has in his bag, which is a bit ironic since he's a part owner of Lynx. His accountant, Edward White, raised $25 million to buy the company in 1996. Clint Eastwood and *Melrose Place*'s Jack Wagner are also investors in the company.

Donald O'Connor

Donald O'Connor, who starred with Gene Kelly in *Singin' in the Rain* and many other classics, has played the game most of his life. "If I had devoted that much time to a computer, I would have taken over the world," says the song-and-dance man, who first learned the game in his youth on the vaudeville circuit. "They used to have trick-shot artists on the bill with us who used to hit the balls up into the balcony. The balls were hard enough to get up to the balcony, but not hard enough to hurt anybody. I picked up a lot of things from those professionals on the road, but I never did learn how to hit the ball off the tee out of the woman's mouth. That I never had the guts to do."

O'Connor made his first movie, *Melody for Two*, in 1937, when he was just eleven. The same year he played in Bing Crosby's first celebrity tournament in Rancho Santa Fe, near San Diego, where he won the putting contest. "I won twenty-four quarts of oil," he says with a laugh. "I had to wait five years before I could use it."

*A*t one point O'Connor was a scratch golfer, but then he started playing for money at Riviera Country Club, which he joined in 1944. "I went right up to a 13," he says. "Everyone else had a phony handicap, so I got one, too."

Usually, O'Connor played for only a few bucks, but he got into one high-stakes game unwittingly in the late forties with actor Bruce Cabot and two other members. "They were a threesome about to tee off and they asked me if I wanted to play," O'Connor recalls. "They said, 'Well, we're playing for one, two, three. Whatever you like to play.' I said, 'Oh, sure, that'd be fine.'"

O'Connor couldn't have played any worse, but it was only after the foursome got into the clubhouse that he found out the "one, two, and threes" had a couple of zeros on them. They were playing five ways for $100 with presses. O'Connor, whose sagging career had yet to be revived by a talking mule in the popular series of *Francis* comedies, was out $2,500. "You know that sinking feeling you get?" he says. "It was terrible. I have a business manager who's giving me twenty-five bucks a week for allowance. I'm trying to figure out how the hell I'm going to get this money to pay these people. I thought about sneaking in the office to get the pink slip to my car."

O'Connor sat there fretting over his fate as the others had a few drinks, when someone suggested double or nothing over "the whiskey route," holes 1, 2, 10, 11, and back up 2 again. "I said, 'Why not?' I didn't have it to pay anyway," he says. "I wasn't drinking in those days, and these guys were stoned. I won the whiskey route and broke even."

Chris O'Donnell

For film star Chris O'Donnell, nirvana isn't a splashy Hollywood premiere. It's thirty-six holes with his childhood buddies at his home course, Shore Acres Club, outside Chicago. "I had one of those days about ten days ago, and I'm still dreaming of it," he says. "There's nobody there playing, we're just whipping around playing each round in, like, three hours and grabbing a cold beer afterwards. That's just the ultimate for me."

When O'Donnell isn't filming such movies as the *Batman* series or *Scent of a Woman*, there's a pretty good chance he's on the golf course. He started playing when he was six, participating in junior programs. At Boston College, his roommates were all on the golf team. "So I've always been around it," says the actor, who's now a 10-handicap. "I love the competitive side of it, playing against your buddies and the fact that you can play anybody using the handicap system. It just gets in your blood. You just can't get enough of it. It's such a hard game that you're always trying to get better at it. Some days you're just hot and it seems so easy. You're hitting every fairway and every green. Then other days you go out there and you can't do anything right."

Even on those days the golf course is a welcome respite, especially for someone who spends a lot of time on location. "It's nice for some-

Chris O'Donnell, Lexus Challenge, La Quinta, California, 1997

one like me who travels around so much. Anywhere I go I can go to a golf course and the smells are the same. It just reminds me of being at home," says O'Donnell, who never got the chance to tee it up with his *Batman* costar, George Clooney. "I feel bad for him that it's come to this, but he's afraid to play me. He beat me in Ping-Pong, he beat me in basketball, but he knows not to mess with me on the golf course."

For his most memorable round, O'Donnell teamed with Arnold Palmer at the Lexus Challenge in December 1996. "It doesn't get much better than that," says O'Donnell, who finished fourth with Arnie. "I was kind of bummed out. I would have loved to have won with Arnie, because he hasn't won in a while. It would just be so cool to be in the record books with Arnie."

Near the start of their first round together at La Quinta's Citrus Course, O'Donnell was going to lay up with his second shot on a par 5. "I was going to hit a 3-iron, then have like an 8-iron in," he says. "He yelled at me, 'Get your 3-wood out, man. Hit it hard. Don't you ever play conservative with me.' I was just trying to manage my game there, and he's like, 'You go for it every hole.' I'm like, 'Allll right.' He must have taken it as an insult that I didn't have faith in him. I can't even remember what happened to the shot, but I'll never forget that. The rest of the trip I was like, 'Well, if I mess up at least Arnie will know I went for it.'"

*F*or the last eight years, in the first week of June O'Donnell and forty of his closest friends make "an annual boys tournament" trip to Florida. In 1997, however, they decided to go international and sixteen of them went to Ireland for a week, playing all the great courses there, such as Ballybunion, Royal County Down, and Tralee.

At Ballybunion, O'Donnell parred the first nine holes, but then failed to break 80, which he's done only once before in his life. "It's classic. I get hot, then I can't keep it together," he says. "I was playing out of my mind. Everyone was bitching at me because my handicap was a 14. I just took so much money from everybody. When I got all the scores in, the handicap dropped very quickly. It's surprising that I could be a 9- or 10-handicap and only broken 80 once. But I've had a lot of low-80 scores at tough tracks."

O'Donnell goes on a lot of golfing junkets where he crams in more golf in a few days than most people play in a month. During a recent trip to San Francisco, he played four rounds at four different courses in three days. The best, though, was one he took to the world's number-one golf course, Pine Valley, in July 1997 with his brother, John, and another friend. In two days, they played 82 holes!

"You always hear so much about the place, and I tell you it is the one place I've been that exceeds all the hype. Most things never live up to it, but this place just blows away anything else," says O'Donnell, who shot a 90-87-86-86. "It's not great, but it's respectable at Pine Valley. It's a fair course with huge fairways and big greens, but if you lose focus for one shot, it kills you. I'd get on a long par 4, cut the corner to where I only had an 8-iron in, hit the approach just off the green, and make double bogey. I made a lot of pars over the course of those four rounds. I think I parred every single hole, but I always had two or three blowup holes."

His biggest number, however, came in the pro shop. "I did some damage in there," says O'Donnell, who practically bought out the store. "I'm wearing my Pine Valley belt right now. I bought a lot of gifts for people. I'm big on the golf gear. I've got a good collection of shirts going. Those are the goodies."

Joe Pesci

Joe Pesci plays golf like one of the intense, mafioso-type characters he portrays so well on screen. On the course, as in many of his roles, he's partial to black clothes, cigars, and cussing. The author of this book was playing with him, along with pro Davis Love III and Hootie and the Blowfish lead singer Darius Rucker, at the 1997 VH1 *Fairway to Heaven* tournament at the Las Vegas Country Club when the actor made a rather liberal interpretation of the one-club rule in the scramble format. On the par-4 4th hole, the chosen drive was in some light rough with some slight tree trouble. Being able to place the ball within a club length eliminated the branch problem, but by the time Pesci took his drop he was a good two to three club lengths away in the fairway. "Joe," the author foolishly tried to point out, "we only get one club."

"Calm down, Tom," he responded in that nasally voice. "This ain't the fuckin' U.S. Open."

You know, he was right. Golf doesn't have to be so serious, especially in a tournament like *Fairway to Heaven*. The showgirl in the G-string and feather headdress carrying the name placard for the group was one indication of that.

Joe Pesci, Lexus Challenge, La Quinta, California, 1997

A 16-handicap, Pesci is a pretty decent golfer capable of holing some putts. He's broken 80 a number of times and used to play to a single-digit handicap a few years back. The game is pure relaxation to him. "It's my salvation," says Pesci, who belongs to three clubs in Los Angeles—Bel-Air, Lakeside, and Sherwood. "Other people go to shrinks, I go to the golf course. It takes my mind off everything else in life."

He started playing when he was a teenager growing up in Belville, New Jersey. The 5′5″ actor weighed 190 pounds then, a good thirty pounds heavier than his current weight. That's probably why he never made it as a caddie. He caddied for one day at Forest Hill Field Club in Bloomfield when he was fifteen. "I put the guy's bag down on the third hole," he recalls. "They said, 'Where you going?' I said, 'I'm going in.' It wasn't worth it when I thought about it."

Pesci doesn't do anything on the course he doesn't want to do. While playing the VH1 tournament, he had a bit of a wait on the 18th tee. A sizeable crowd gathered before the fairway finally cleared. Pesci took a furious whack at his monogrammed Maxfli and hit the ball right into a giant cooler at the end of the tee box. The ball came ricocheting backward, ending up twenty yards behind him. Disgusted, he got in his cart and headed in. He had had enough.

Tom Poston

Known for his roles on such sitcoms as *Mork and Mindy* and *Bob Newhart*, Tom Poston plays to about a 16-handicap and belongs to Bel-Air Country Club. "My wife says I play day and night," he says. "But it's really an exaggeration. I don't think I've played at night more than half a dozen times all year."

In truth, Poston gets out about once a week, but golf just isn't a challenge for him as it is for everyone else. "Golf is the easiest thing in the world," he says. "You only have two things to worry about: distance and direction. If you can't handle those two things, get off the course."

The man is so haunted by the game that he has a recurring nightmare about it. "It's my turn and I can't find a place to tee up the ball," he says. "People are waiting or they're gone. There's a tree in my way or a branch, so I move it and then there's a wall. Then I move it and I can't see the green, so I move it again. It's just so frustrating." Asked if he's told a doctor about it, Poston replies, "No, his handicap is worse than mine."

But seriously, folks, when Poston thinks back on all his rounds, his fondest memories involve playing with his son, Jason, over the last twenty-five years. "It's just the joy of my life to know that we've been able to spend that much time together doing something that we love," Tom says. "We've played all over the country, because I used to travel doing theater. We've played hundreds of rounds together."

Jason is a big hitter who first outhit his dad when he was sixteen at Edmonton Country Club while Tom was touring in Canada. "We were more or less at the same place on the hole, and I hit a nine short and he hit a wedge over the green," Tom recalls. "I said, 'Whoops, that's it.' I don't think he paid much attention to it, but it was very obvious to me that the king is dead, long live the king."

*P*oston's best round came when he shot a 69 at Lexington Golf and Country Club in Virginia in the seventies. "I had a lower handicap then, but not anywhere near that low," he recalls, noting that he shot 31 on the front. "I was pissed, because I didn't make the twenty-foot putt on 9. On the back I thought, 'Now I've finally found my game. I knew it should be like this. I probably will improve now.' I knew the shots I missed on the front and I thought I could do better than that." He ended up shooting a 38 on the back and never came close to shooting in the 60s again. "I went up from there. I thought I knew what I was doing. I certainly don't know now."

Maury Povich

Although talk-show host Maury Povich didn't start playing golf until age thirty, the game has always been a big part of his life. That's because his dad, longtime Washington *Post* sports columnist Shirley Povich, came to his livelihood through the game. As a youth growing up in Bar Harbor, Maine, the elder Povich caddied for *Post* owner Ned McClain, who summered there. When Shirley graduated from high school, McClain gave him a job at his paper.

Now ninety-two, the senior Povich still hacks it around with his caddie swing. "He tells everybody he lost his clubhead speed at eighty-nine," says Maury, a scratch player who belongs to Hollywood Country Club in Deal, New Jersey. "To show you how avid a golfer I am, I will finish work around one or two in the afternoon, drive an hour and a half to Hollywood, and then drive back to the city about three days a week."

Povich is also a member at Woodmont Country Club, outside Washington, D.C., where he's won the club championship numerous times, most recently in 1996 when he successfully defended his championship against a twenty-three-year-old. "It was one of my proudest moments, because I won the thirty-six-hole final 1-up and I was 1 over par," he recalls. "I was never more than 1-up. I got up and down the first four holes, just to remain even. I went 1-up around 7 and we halved 8 through 18 in the morning. Then, in the afternoon, we pushed every hole, so I was 1-up on the 36th hole after he missed an eighteen-foot birdie to tie me. It was a grueling, grinding match. It reminded me that this is the way golf was invented to be played."

*A*fter winning four straight club championships at Hollywood from 1992 to 1996, Povich has now retired from club events to concentrate on playing in the U.S. Senior Open and U.S. Senior Amateur. He almost qualified for the former in June 1997 at Mountain Ridge Country Club in New Jersey. With 100 players vying for three spots, Povich was in one of the final groups when he came to the 17th hole 2 under on the par-71 course. A 68 and 69 had already been posted. If he could par in, he'd make it. He finished 8, 6, after duck-hooking both his drives out-of-bounds.

"As it turned out, 71 played off," says Povich, who called his teacher, Peter Kostis, when he got home. "He said, 'Sixty-nine is not your comfort level. You haven't been in competition like that enough. If you had parred 17, you'd have made 9 on 18.' My comfort level is 72, 74. My last mountain to climb is mental. He's trying to make me believe that I have the talent to compete on this level, but something inside me still says I'm not ready or I don't want to."

A collector of golf memorabilia, Povich owns one of the 28 copies known to exist in the world of *The Goff,* the first book ever written about the game, published in 1743. He also has a rare square-toed iron from the 1700s, which he occasionally uses to chip with on the hole he built behind his weekend home in New Jersey, much to the amusement of his nonplaying wife, newswoman Connie Chung.

"She likes me to play," he says. "She knows I take great joy in it. Connie knew long ago, before we ever got married, that I was a golf addict. I recommend that all diseased golfers make sure that their girlfriends or wives know this well before there are rings on fingers. Because if you get this disease after you get married, there is big trouble ahead."

Randy Quaid

*P*robably the only actor to get a role on the *strength* of his golfing skills is Randy Quaid. He auditioned for the lead role of U.S. Open hopeful Kenny Lee in HBO's 1988 adaptation of Dan Jenkins's novel, *Dead Solid Perfect*, at MountainGate Country Club in Los Angeles. Quaid, a 5-handicap, did pretty well considering he struggled with his vision.

"I had just gotten some contacts and had never worn them playing," recalls Quaid, who was playing with the head of HBO and the film's director. "I was sort of playing half blind, but I didn't want them to see me wearing glasses or they might not have given me the part. Kenny Lee didn't wear glasses. My first hole I was in the greenside bunker. I was worried that the sand might hit me in the eyes and make the situation even worse."

Fortunately, that wasn't the case. Quaid ended up shooting 78 that day, hitting "a lot of really good shots," including one seventy-yard bunker shot that he put five feet from the hole. As every fan of the film knows, Quaid got the job.

*R*andy and his brother Dennis have a lot of heated matches against each other, even though Dennis just started playing about five years ago (Randy started at age eleven). Beating his younger brother is one of the things that Randy enjoys most about the game. "All the brotherly rivalry and competitiveness really has a place," says Randy, who belongs to both Bel-Air Country Club and Winged Foot Golf Club, in New York. "Dennis is not a needler. I'm more of one. He's very passive on the course, but he's not as bad as he used to be. When he first started playing, he was very serious. I mean, you couldn't even talk to him."

Robert Redford

Robert Redford doesn't play much golf these days, but he liked to when he was growing up in Los Angeles and early on in his career. One day, he was playing a round at Bel-Air County Club as the guest of football legend Tom Harmon. In Bel-Air's book, *A Living Legend*, Harmon said that Redford played so poorly the first three holes that he was embarrassed. Then he birdied the toughest hole on the course, the uphill par-4 4th, which runs along the club's boundary, and the par-3 5th.

"You sprang to life," Harmon told him. A sheepish Redford then made a confession. "Once upon a time there'd been a kid with two clubs who shinnied over the fence on many occasions to play these same two holes. That kid was me. At last, I get to play the whole 18."

Pamela Reed

*P*amela Reed, who costarred with Arnold Schwarzenegger in *Kindergarten Cop*, has a very soft spot in her heart for the game of golf. That's because her father, Vernie, a union official and single-digit handicap who died twenty years ago, taught her to play. He made her her first set of clubs when she was six. "I grew up swinging in the backyard with him and going out with him once in a while," says Reed, who went with her father to Congressional Country Club when she was eleven to see Ken Venturi win the U.S. Open in 1964. "I still clearly remember that periscope that allowed me to look over the crowd."

A few years later, her dad took her to a union convention at the Greenbrier Hotel in West Virginia, the home of Sam Snead. One day, he took her out on the course with him. A parade of carts lined the first tee as groups of foursomes waited their turn to tee off. Not only was Reed the only kid, but she was also the only female.

"I was *really* nervous," she recalls. "My dad just looked at me and said softly, 'Just keep your head down and your eye on the ball. You'll be fine.' One of the guys from our foursome stepped up—slice. The next guy hooked it. Then it was my turn. I hit it right down the center of the fairway. I will always remember the look on my father's face. He was a very quiet, calm man, but he looked at me with such love at that moment. I have carried that in my heart to this day, that moment with my father."

With a couple of children of her own now, Reed, who's a 25-handicap, doesn't get to play as much as she'd like. "It's hard to get out, but I love it," she says. "I love it mostly because it brings my father back to me."

Joe Regalbutto

O n *Murphy Brown* he plays the put-upon Frank Fontana, but on the golf course Joe Regalbutto is a take-no-prisoners kind of guy. At his home course, Riviera Country Club, he won the 1997 net club championship in a seventy-two-hole stroke-play tournament. "It was really exciting, because I played against a couple of tough guys, a couple of known sandbaggers," says the actor, a 7-handicap who shot 78-78 the final two rounds. "The 20-handicappers are the ones you have to watch out for. It was really fun. There are no gimmes. It's a riot. You stand over a two-and-a-half-footer and you pray it into the hole."

Regalbutto trailed the leader by two shots heading into the final round. Before heading out, someone told him, "Tell yourself you can win this thing. Play smart, but aggressively." The advice would come in handy. After shooting a 2-over 37 on the front, he had picked up only one stroke and thought to himself, "Oh, this is going to be a long friggin' day."

The turning point came at the dogleg-left, par-4 13th. Regalbutto pushed his tee shot into the stand of eucalyptus trees on the right, leaving him a low cut if he wanted to go for the green. "It's a shot I'd been practicing a lot," he recalls. "But I'm looking right into a barranca and out-of-bounds. If I don't hit it right, I'm looking at a disaster, so I decided to take my pitching wedge and chip out. I took the pitching wedge out and I said, 'You know what, damn it? Play aggressive. You know how to make that shot. You can . . . make . . . that . . . shot. You've practiced it a million times.'"

He put the wedge back, pulled out his 5-iron, and ended up two feet off the green. He chipped to a foot and made par. "It really gave me confidence," he says. "That was really exciting, to imagine a shot and then pull it off. That's when the golf really starts to get fun, when you start getting away from 'Please, God, let me just hit the ball,' to 'I'm gonna cut this one, I'm gonna hook this one.' When you start to get a glimpse of that, you realize how much there is to it."

*R*egalbutto has been playing for only five years, but he's a real student of the game who loves to practice. He takes a lot of lessons from noted instructor and former tour player Mac O'Grady, who had the actor caddie for him at the 1996 Hartford Open. On the first hole, a straightaway par 4, Dennis Watson teed off first and hit his shot fifty yards out-of-bounds. "Mac turns around, gives me a look, and goes, 'Oh, man,'" Regalbutto recalls. "This is my first caddying experience, and here it is in a pro tournament. I am scared to death. I have no clue what I'm doing."

Glen Day hit next, ripping one down the middle. "Mac gets up, he hits the ball seventy yards out-of-bounds left," Regalbutto recalls. "And I'm going, 'Oh, God, why is this happening to me?' And Mac says, very quietly, 'Give me another ball,' which he hit down the middle. I was dying. I had eighteen holes to go, plus a whole other day. But it was fun. You get a little glimpse of what these guys are going through. Being inside the ropes and watching these guys who do it for their livings, it's the same humiliation we feel, the same pain of not making the shot that you anticipated. It's as though you've swung the club."

Regalbutto also caddied for O'Grady in both the regional and sectional qualifying for the 1997 U.S. Open, but he's not about to switch careers anytime soon. "I don't ever volunteer anything," he says. "I know what a good pet feels like. 'Here I am.' You don't want to be the one who's responsible. 'Whoops, I was two yards short. You're now in the water. I'm so sorry.' I have a day job, so I don't need to get too wrapped up in it."

Darius Rucker, VH1 Fairway to Heaven tournament, Las Vegas, 1997

Darius Rucker

hough he didn't get serious about golf until four years ago, Darius
Rucker, the lead singer of Hootie and the Blowfish, first played
the game twenty years ago as a fourteen-year-old growing up in
South Carolina. It's one of his fondest golfing memories and one
that's still fresh in his mind. He'd often be at the home of his best
friend, Rick Johannes, when Rick and his dad would go play golf at
the Charleston Air Force Base course. "I think his dad got tired of
me leaving and he said, 'Hey, c'mon, we're going to play golf,'"
Rucker recalls. "That was the first time I played. Ever since then I've
been hooked. I remember it vividly. I probably shot a 130, but we had
a blast. Captain Johannes was such a huge figure in my life, so playing golf with him was just awesome. Every time they went from then
on, he took me along. He taught me how to play. It was pretty cool."

ucker doesn't get to play as much as he'd like when he's on tour,
but he more than makes up for it when he's home at the Wild
Dunes golf complex in South Carolina. He gets out four times a
week, often playing 36 holes a day. "It's so challenging. You think
you've got it down, then you go out and shoot 98," says the singer,
who came close to his goal of breaking 80 recently in Michigan.

"Dean, our bass player, was playing with me. After 15 he said, 'Dude, if you get three bogeys, you're going to shoot a 79.' I got two bogeys and a double. My head was totally gone on the 18th tee. I couldn't have hit that drive straight if my life depended on it. I wanted that 79 so bad."

*I*ronically, his finest golfing moment came on one of his more embarrassing days. He was playing with the knicker-attired pro Payne Stewart in the Phoenix Open a few years ago and having a dreadful day. By the end, a totally frustrated Rucker, who had been topping his shots all day, stood in the middle of the 18th fairway 160 yards from the pin. Thousands of fans surrounded the hole. Stewart surveyed the throng and joked to him, "You've got to get this in the air, man." He got the ball airborne, all right, lipping out a 6-iron. "The ball stopped three inches from the cup," he says, cracking a big smile. "The crowd went nuts. I felt like the luckiest man in America."

Randolph Scott

Randolph Scott became a film star after meeting Howard Hughes on a golf course. He went on to become the prototype of the Hollywood cowboy star: tall, rugged, and weathered. He hit his peak in the fifties in a series of rough B Westerns, such as *Buchanan Rides Alone*.

Scott retired in the early sixties as one of Hollywood's richest men, with savvy investments in oil, real estate, and stock. But when he applied for membership at the Los Angeles Country Club, which traditionally turns away screen personalities, he was met with some resistance.

"But aren't you an actor?" he was asked.

"No," Scott responded without missing a beat, "and I've got seventy-six pictures to prove it."

The actor died in 1987, and no one knows if the tale is true. But the club's restrictions remain. Ronald Reagan is the only member with an acting background, and he had to become governor of California before he was accepted.

Jonathan Silverman

The Single Guy's Jonathan Silverman isn't much of a golfer; he plays only a couple of times a year. But he does have the dubious distinction of having had a lead role in one of the worst golf movies of all time, 1988's *Caddyshack II*. "It's not even on my résumé," he says. "We hoped it would be half as funny as the original, but it was nowhere near that. It was three incredibly silly months on a golf course, but it's a giant piece of crap."

In the movie, which is a lot like the original—only without the laughs—Silverman plays a caddie who substitutes for an injured Chevy Chase in a golf match for ownership of the club. Silverman was a complete beginner when he got the role and had to undergo three weeks of intense, er, rehearsal.

"All that amounted to was me working with a golf pro every day developing my swing," he says, noting that no double was used. "They just needed a couple of decent shots of me swinging. It wasn't anything too difficult, a couple of putts and, of course, a lot of acting. Ironically, I worked so hard on perfecting at least a decent golf swing so golfers who would be watching the movie would not question the fact that I would be a golfer."

But by the time Silverman had to shoot his crucial on-course scenes, the crew was in such close proximity that plastic balls were used. "You just had to loft it up a little bit out of frame to make it look like you hit a decent one, but in reality it goes about ten feet," he says. "If you used a legitimate swing the ball would go nowhere, so you had to alter your swing entirely. So all those lessons really went down the drain. But that's showbiz."

Will Smith

One of Hollywood's hottest stars after successive hits like *Independence Day* and *Men in Black*, Will Smith is good friends with golf's biggest draw, Tiger Woods. The actor is a self-described "golf junkie" and a 14-handicap. The two superstars have teed it up together a couple of times. When they played in South Carolina not long after Woods won the Masters, Smith took it easy on him. "I figured he was young, and I didn't want to go out there beatin' on the boy like that," he said recently. "So I let him take me by twenty-six strokes."

A few months before that, Smith had taken Woods to North Ranch Country Club, one of the two clubs to which the actor belongs, north of Los Angeles. Just as Tiger was about to tee off, Smith called up his teaching pro, Ron Del Barrio, on his cellular phone. "He said, 'Listen to this,'" Del Barrio says. "He held his phone out and I hear this big *swooosh!!!!* It was Tiger hitting his drive."

Del Barrio used to work with Smith at a public course in the San Fernando Valley, but "it just got too crazy." Now they can work together in private in Smith's backyard, where he built a par-3 hole with two tee boxes, one from ninety yards and the other from 160. "He's so serious about learning, nobody can be around," the pro says.

"He'll want to learn for eight hours straight. He just plunked down $200,000 to join Sherwood Country Club, so he's getting pretty screwed up."

"I'm hooked really badly," Smith has admitted. "It's, like, the best metaphor for life that there is in sports. Through those eighteen holes, you're up, you're down. You hit a bad shot, you're out. But your next shot is incredible, and you're back in it again. You can golf with someone and tell what kind of person they are without ever hearing them talk. When it's a beautiful day, you get out and drive around in your little cart and look at the water and the mountains. It's just a really peaceful experience."

Smith is friends with casino mogul Steve Wynn and travels often to Las Vegas to play Wynn's stupendous private course, Shadow Creek Country Club, where a round of golf costs $1,000. With a huge suite provided to him gratis, Smith brings along a couple of friends, of course, to join him for a couple days of thirty-six-hole marathons. One time recently when he was playing with Del Barrio and one of his costars from *The Fresh Prince of Bel-Air*, Alfie Ribeiro, Smith was unaware of his score. Not coincidentally, he was having the best round of his life. On the 17th tee, he asked Del Barrio how he was doing. "You're 4 over," he said to a disbelieving Smith, who responded, "Wait a second. You're not telling me I can shoot 76 out here?" Said Del Barrio: "That's exactly what I'm telling you. Just hit fairways and greens."

Smith finished triple, triple. "He had a brain fart," the pro recalls. "He was so scared, he didn't know what to do and proceeded to hit about seven balls in the water. He shot 81 for the day and he could have shot 74, because the day before he had shot 2 under on the last three holes. They're pretty easy. But he's nuts about it. When he went to Spain for the press junket for *Men in Black*, he was begging me to go. He was like, 'All we'll do is play golf, all we'll do is play golf.' They're all nuts like that."

Tommy Smothers

Comedian Tommy Smothers started playing golf in 1984 when he and his brother, Dick, were headlining in Las Vegas. "He said, 'You look like shit, you look sick,'" Tommy recalls. "I was staying up till four in the morning, hanging out with musicians and comedians and dancers. He bought me some clubs and took me out to a golf course and set me up. I've been playing ever since. I started going to bed right after the show and started waking up early to go work on my golf. It changed my life."

Now he belongs to two country clubs, Wilshire in Los Angeles and Santa Rosa in northern California, and gets out about once or twice a week. Smothers, a 15-handicap who's broken 80 twice, even has his wife, Marcy, playing. She's more rabid about the game than he is. "I call her a golf slut—lovingly—because she cannot pass a driving range," says Tommy. "She's really into it."

Smother's signature prop, of course, is the yo-yo. And if you see it at a golf tournament, you know he's not playing too well. "If my golf swing isn't very good that day, I will take out the yo-yo to take the pressure off," he says. "It takes the onus off my golf. People start laughing. If I'm striking the ball well, I invariably do not take it out."

The yo-yo was in full view when he was playing with Mark Calcavecchia at the 1991 Nissan Open at Riviera Country Club in Los Angeles. Smothers will often "putt" the yo-yo. He makes it sleep and then plumb-bobs with it before gently placing the spinning orb on the green, where it takes off for the hole. Usually the yo-yo stops well short of the hole or goes whizzing well past. "It's hard to control," he says. But at Riviera he sunk it from twenty-seven feet. "The crowd went crazy, screamed like it was a hole in one. Mark walked it off. He couldn't believe it. That's the only time it's ever gone in for me, and I do it almost every hole."

Sylvester Stallone

Many Hollywood celebrities are obsessed with the game, but their fanaticism pales in comparison to that of Sylvester Stallone. His devotion stems from the challenge the game provides. "Nothing's more important than golf," says Ron Del Barrio, Stallone's personal pro from 1990 to 1996. "He's as addicted as I've ever seen. He's got to master it and improve. The fact that he, Rambo, could not master the game frustrated the hell out of him."

Stallone plays to about a 10-handicap but wants to get down to scratch. To that end, "He doesn't go anywhere without golf being included in some way," says Del Barrio, who even coached the actor at three A.M. on the rooftop of a downtown Los Angeles building, where Stallone was filming scenes for *Demolition Man* in 1993. "As soon as the director would shout, 'Cut!' he would go straight to the driving net. He had on his futuristic costume and these black boots. He'd have the catering people bring dinner to the driving net. Or we'd go into his camper to watch videos and instructional tapes. He wouldn't take phone calls. Any spare second he had away from the actual camera would be spent on golf. If it wasn't physically, we were talking about the mental aspects of the game."

Indeed, on a trip aboard a chartered Gulfstream G-4 to the Caribbean for the 1992 Christmas holidays, all he did with Del Barrio during the long flight was work on "visualization." The whole trip, of course, revolved around golf. Stallone had chartered a

200-foot yacht and invited three other couples along. "The captain said, 'Okay, the travel times start at seven in the morning. Each island's about three hours apart. . . .' Sylvester said, 'No, no, we travel when we sleep, so that when I get up we play golf,'" Del Barrio recalls. "The captain said, 'We usually don't travel at night.' He goes, 'You do now.' The damn boat was rocking so much, everybody was sick and puking when they're trying to sleep. But he didn't care, as long as we could golf the next morning."

They played golf on just about every course in the West Indies, including Robert Trent Jones Jr.'s renowned layout on the tiny island of Nevis. The weather was a bit humid, but Stallone was having a terrific round. He came to the 13th hole, a par 5, only 2 over and wanted to reach the green in two. "He swung so hard and the humidity was so bad that the club flew out of his hands," Del Barrio recalls. "As it was in midair and everybody's looking at the club, he runs over to me and grabs my club. His club breaks a window in this condo. This lady sticks her head out yelling in some foreign language, and I'm standing there naked without a club. Then he made me go claim 'my' driver. Bastard."

Stallone's best round was in 1992 at difficult Wood Ranch Country Club, north of Los Angeles, where he shot a 74 from the tips. "I was shocked," Del Barrio says. "He was so elated, he wanted to buy everyone whatever they wanted. 'Here's a Rolex. Take it. Who cares? I just shot 74.' He said it was better than the Oscar he won for *Rocky*. He said, 'You can have it if I can just shoot this number all the time.' He was beside himself for a month."

Alan Thicke

Alan Thicke used to star on the NBC sitcom *Growing Pains* with fellow golf nut Joanna Kerns, but don't remind him. "She actually told the world on *Regis and Kathie Lee* that she beat me," says Thicke, a 19-handicap who's been playing about five years. "She's a good golfer, but I think she could have kept that in the family."

Thicke likes many things about the game, one of which is that "you get to commune with a lot of friends without having to have them over for dinner," he says. "My favorite thing about golf is that you get to start a new hole every seven strokes. I play Canadian golf, which means we're just happy to be outdoors."

At the 1995 Lexus Challenge, Raymond Floyd's celebrity tournament held in La Quinta, California, each December, Thicke was paired with Jack Nicklaus. They came to a 200-yard par 3 over water. Nicklaus hit first. Kerplunk! A stricken-looking Thicke then stepped up to the tee nervously clutching a 5-wood. "It was the most pressure I've ever had in golf," he says. "What do I do? I missed a hole in one by a foot. I lipped the cup." Nicklaus gave him a smile and said, "Lucky shot, Canadian."

After Thicke managed to cajole his one-foot birdie putt into the cup, the team wound up with a net 1 on the hole because he also stroked and went on to win the pro-am part of the tournament. Afterward, Nicklaus sent him a fabulous set of clubs from his company. "He was such a great guy," Thicke says. "The Bear was a pussycat."

*T*here have been many humorous moments in Thicke's golfing life, but perhaps the funniest came at the present-day incarnation of Bing Crosby's celebrity tournament, which is held in Winston-Salem, North Carolina. Thicke sliced a 3-wood from the fairway on a par 5 into a home adjoining the course. The ball ended up in the family's Jacuzzi while they were in it! "They were laughing, and I just said, 'Mind if I play through?'" he recalls. "If there's water I'll find it, even a Jacuzzi. I spray it around a bit. It takes a lot of balls to golf the way I do."

Jack Wagner

*J*ack Wagner of *Melrose Place* is the best celebrity golfer playing the game today. In addition to winning the Bel-Air Country Club club championship four times now, he's also won more than $150,000 on the Celebrity Players Tour, having turned professional in 1992. His first win as a pro came in 1994 at Barton Creek in Austin, Texas, when he shot 8 under par over three days to collect $20,000.

Playing in the last group with the leader, former major-league pitcher Rick Rhoden, Wagner trailed by five shots going into the final round. By the 17th hole, he was still three shots down. Standing on the tee of the 205-yard par 3 at 6 under par, Wagner thought to himself, "How am I going to win this tournament?" A good start was to birdie the hole, which he did after rolling in a twenty-footer. When Rhoden bogeyed, his lead was cut to one.

The 18th at Barton Creek is a par 5 that's reachable in two, but there are hazards lurking left off the tee and in front of the green. Rhoden pulled his drive into the trouble and wound up making a bogey, while Wagner knocked it on the green in two. He two-putted for birdie and won the tournament by a stroke. In two holes, he made up four strokes.

Jack Wagner, Isuzu Celebrity Golf Championship, Lake Tahoe, 1997

*A*s a pro, Wagner is no longer eligible to play in one of his favorite events, the AT&T Pebble Beach National Pro-Am, but he's not too upset since he already won that in 1990 with John Cook as his partner. It was a very sentimental victory, given that his dad, Pete, an auto salesman who taught him to play while Jack was growing up in Missouri, had died just a few months before. "He's the main reason that I got into golf," says Wagner, who's a part owner of Lynx golf club company. "My son, who we named Pete after my dad, was born right before the golf tournament, so it was one of those give-and-take kind of deals."

Wagner played the tournament as a 4-handicap and ended up shooting just about even par on his own ball the last two days at Pebble Beach. On the final day playing with Paul Azinger, who was battling Cook for the individual title, Wagner birdied 14 and 15 before parring 16 and 17, getting up and down on the latter. CBS captured his exploits every step of the way. Cook birdied 18 to give them the win, though he lost the main tournament to Azinger.

To be right in the thick of it with the leaders on a Sunday afternoon in a PGA Tour event is a huge thrill for anyone, Wagner included. "As an amateur to be paired with these champions as they play Pebble Beach was a lot of fun," he says. "Davis Love was right behind us, and all these guys are vying for the championship. I'm right in there playing pretty good golf with these pros. That probably is the most memorable win for me."

*W*agner won one tournament in 1997 on the Celebrity Players Tour, in Puerto Rico, and might have won the association's biggest event at Lake Tahoe in July, the Isuzu Celebrity Championship, were it not for a bizarre penalty in the first round. On the 8th hole, a par-4 dogleg right, Wagner's drive came to rest by a big pine tree in the middle of the fairway. He accidentally nicked the tree in his backswing, causing some bark to fall off. He stopped his shot, readdressed the ball, and knocked it on the green. As they were checking their scorecards after the round, one of his playing companions, NFL quarterback Steve Bartkowski, said to him, "I think some bark came off that tree. We ought to get a ruling on that."

So the two of them and a couple of officials rode out there in carts to reenact the event. They ruled that Wagner was improving his lie (had he not stopped his swing that wouldn't have been the case), turning his 69 into a 71. "Those trees have flaky bark," says Wagner, who finished six strokes back of the winner, Rick Rhoden. "If I wouldn't have gotten dinged with that two-stroke penalty, I might have played a little differently."

Robert Wagner

Robert Wagner, who has starred in such TV series as *It Takes a Thief* and *Hart to Hart*, became an actor because of golf. In his youth, Wagner used to caddie at Bel-Air Country Club for the likes of Clark Gable, Jimmy Stewart, and Cary Grant. "I was starstruck," he recalls. "I wanted to be in the movies." Gable, a 13-handicap who once had a hole-in-one at the 200-yard 13th, gave Wagner his acting start when he personally took him over to MGM in 1948.

"He was busy all the time, so he didn't have a lot of time to devote to his game, but he did enjoy it," says Wagner, a 12-handicap who's a founding member of Sherwood Country Club, an extremely posh club north of Los Angeles that attracts a lot of celebrities. "I've been so blessed to have this game in my life. It's taken me to some of the most beautiful places on earth and introduced me to many great people. It's the only sport I know of where you can remember a shot you hit ten years ago."

Or thirty years ago. In 1967, the first year Wagner played in Crosby's Clambake, he had his first and last hole-in-one, at the then 5th hole at Cypress Point Club. For the 170-yard shot, Wagner used a 6-iron. The ball landed about fifteen feet short and just trickled in over the edge. "What a time to get it," he says. "Can you imagine? And after that I couldn't have hit you with a golf bag."

When the tournament was over, Wagner had another unforgettable moment at Cypress. He and a longtime friend, celebrity journalist Jim Bacon, caught the course early one morning that was right out of some golfer's dream. "We were the only people on the golf course," Wagner recalls. "It was one of those mornings when the fog raised, and the deer came out, and the sun was coming down on the ocean. It was a day I'll never forget. It was so memorable. Whenever I see Jim, we always talk about that time. We saw one of the greatest golf courses in the world at the time it was perfect. It was so ethereal. It was one of God's moments for golf."

Needless to say, they both play inspired rounds.

Johnny Weissmuller

Swimming wasn't the only sport at which Johnny Weissmuller excelled. He was a terrific golfer who once shot 63 at his home course, Lakeside Golf Club, and had five holes in one. He expected so much of his game that if he didn't break 70, he admitted in Lakeside's fiftieth-anniversary book, he'd often break a club (or two). One of his regular playing partners, Mickey Rooney, also had a bit of a temper, and was known to throw a lot of clubs.

Weissmuller knew how to have fun on the course, though. When he played Bel-Air Country Club, where some of his *Tarzan* movies had been shot, he would climb up on a huge rock surrounded by a thicket (dubbed "the jungle" by members) and give a Tarzan yell that would echo throughout the course.

One year there was a tournament on Catalina Island that about twenty guys from Lakeside played in. Many of them went over on Weissmuller's fifty-five-foot sailboat. "I was snoozing on deck, and as I stood up a giant swell hit the boat and I went overboard," he recalled in Lakeside's book. "This was one time my Tarzan yell didn't do me one bit of good. Boy, did I yell. Well, to cut the story down to two reels, I swam and swam. It didn't scare me, because I knew the channel very well, but there were sharks all over the place. I could see the lights of Avalon about five miles away, so I headed for shore. In the meantime, my skipper discovered he'd lost me and was searching like mad, circling and circling in the black of night. He was going out of his gourd. I was waiting on the dock when the poor frantic guy got to Avalon. I said, 'Where the hell have you been?' He was speechless."

Weissmuller went on to win the tournament—swimmingly, you might say.

Andy Williams

*N*ow living in Branson, Missouri, where he owns the Moon River Theater, Andy Williams plays golf just about every day, but he doesn't get to gamble for big money as he did when he lived in Los Angeles. "You're lucky to get a $2 nassau here," says the crooner, a 15-handicap who used to play a lot of golf at Riviera Country Club with producer Pierre Cossette. "We used to bet $1,000 a hole. I lost big this one time because he chipped one in on the last hole for $5,000."

Williams got him back but good another time. Cossette started to relieve himself behind their cart right in the middle of a fairway. A group of ladies was on an adjoining hole. "I said, 'Pierre, you can't do that,'" Williams recalls. "He said, 'Ah, nobody can see me,' so I stepped on the gas and started singing 'Moon River' at the top of my lungs. And all these ladies looked over and saw him standing there with his dick in his hands."

*A*ndy Williams hosted the San Diego Open for about twenty years, but he never got used to playing in front of people, especially on the first tee. "You're afraid you're going to whiff it or do something dumb," he says. "People see you up there. 'Oh, Andy's got his own tournament. Go get 'em, Andy!' They think if you're an entertainer and you're well known, God, you must be a good golfer, then you hit a bad ball and they all groan."

One of his stranger moments came at Bob Hope's Desert Classic in the early eighties. Paired with Lee Trevino, Williams was getting the kinks out on the practice range at Indian Wells Country Club when he heard his name being paged—he was to report to the first tee right away. He rushed over and Trevino said, "You better hurry up, we've all hit." A jittery Williams, who was extra excited to be playing with Trevino, quickly put a ball down and hit a good shot right down the middle over water.

When they got to where his ball should be, they couldn't find it anywhere. "I watch everybody's ball," Trevino said to him. "I know where everybody is. You should be right out here and you're not here. The only thing here is a range ball."

Eventually, Williams realized that he had hit a range ball off the first tee in his hurried state. "It had two black stripes around it and I never even noticed it, I was so nervous," he says. "Lee started laughing. He saw Palmer at the next tee and he yelled over, 'Hey, Arnie, Andy was so nervous he hit a range ball off the first tee.' And you hear him laughing. 'Ha-ha-ha.' Then you hear somebody laughing three holes farther down. The story got around the whole course. Lee can't get over the fact that I hit a ball and didn't even notice that there were two big black stripes around it."

*W*illiams's most humiliating moment in a celebrity tournament came at the Crosby in the early sixties. He was on the 18th green at Pebble Beach lining up a thirty-foot putt. The TV cameras were on him, Bing was up in the booth waving at him, and an attentive gallery awaited his stroke. "I got over the ball and I got dizzy," he recalls. "The adrenaline was leaving my body. I was about to faint. Finally, I had to stroke this putt. I was so nervous that I hit my toe with my putter and it knocked the ball ninety degrees the other way. There must have been two or three thousand people around the green. They all went, 'Ugggghhhh,' at the same time. It sounded like a big puke. I looked up and nobody was looking at me—Bing, the camera people were all looking the other way. It was horrible."

Scott Wolf

One of the stars of Fox's popular drama *Party of Five*, Scott Wolf suffered perhaps Hollywood's worst golf tragedy. His story would be utterly hysterical were it not for the high probability that it could happen to anyone who plays in golf tournaments. As Ben Hogan once said, there's golf and then there's tournament golf.

Wolf was a senior at George Washington University who had tried out for the golf team his final year at school and made it. The team's first tournament, an NCAA Division I stroke-play event, was held at Ocean Point Golf Links in Fripp Island, South Carolina, and required a lot of accuracy off the tee. Other than high school golf, Wolf had never played any kind of competitive golf, but he got off to a good start and was 1 under after four holes.

The 5th hole, a dogleg-left par 4, had water running all along the right side. Wolf pushed his drive right and his ball went into the hazard. After taking a drop and hitting 3, he hit his next shot into the water to the right of the green. "I was now hitting 5, and at this point I sort of went into a golf coma," he says. "I wound up with a 10 on the hole. This was the first time that it wasn't 'X' on the scorecard or I could pick up. The rest of the round, I was afraid to take the club back."

He was in the middle of every golfer's worst nightmare.

Wolf started playing when he was growing up in West Orange, New Jersey, where he caddied and played number one on his high school golf team. He didn't play his first three years in college, and as his senior year was rolling around, he started thinking about what he was going to do with his life. "Something came upon me and I had the delusion for a while, 'What if I could be a professional golfer?'" he recalls. "I had no perspective or awareness of what it took, the physical and mental ability it takes to be successful on that level, or just to be able to compete on that level."

Over the summer, he assiduously applied himself to the task at hand, taking lessons at his dad's club, Cresmont Country Club, and practicing every day. "I was challenging myself to see how good I could get," says Wolf, who began the summer as a 14-handicap and ended it as a 6. "I couldn't get enough of it. For the first time I was standing over the ball not so much wondering where it would go, but how it would get where I wanted it to go. It was the first time in my life that I felt some sort of control, and the game became much more specific and creative. It wasn't just try and hit it straight. It was the first time I was able to play with some imagination. And I loved it even more for that."

When he returned to school, he tried out for the team, shooting 76 with the coach and earning a scholarship. There was no fall program, however, and Wolf was more interested in having fun than working on his game on his own. He hadn't touched a club for six months when he found himself on a bus headed for South Carolina and disaster in March of 1990.

"I didn't have any idea what I was involved in," he says. "It had gotten easy for me to go out and feel confident over the ball when I was at my dad's course, where there's no giant leader board at the end that was going to post scores."

After the traumatic 5th hole, Wolf took to punching 7-irons off the tee just so he could find his ball. "It got so bad that even my competitors, the guys I was playing with, were trying to help me out," he says. "They were like, 'Just take it easy. You were making the swing early on. Just make the swing.' But I was shell-shocked. It was as hard an athletic experience as I've ever had, just in terms of being so unbelievably out of control and having so little access to the ability that I had to swing the golf club because I was so thrown mentally."

When he got to the 18th hole, he had a twenty-five-footer to break 100. He drained it and got really pumped up over it. "I *really* did not want to be up on the big board with triple digits," he says. "I did not want to have 100 up there next to my name. My coach comes running over because he sees me kind of celebrating and thinks I'm going to be leading the tournament. I said, 'That just saved me a 99.' For some reason, they kept me on the team."

But he was never the same. "I got terrified of what could happen if it went wrong," he says. "But it has taught me a lot of great lessons, in terms of the way I want to live my life and the best way to approach things. It's why I've recently found the game again and why I've started to play a lot. Before that 10 on that par 4 I was focused on the process, how I felt over the ball. As soon as I was focused on where the ball was going, I was afraid of every other possibility."

Wolf, who's now a 12-handicap and Lakeside Golf Club member, has learned, paradoxically, that you achieve control only when you surrender it. "For me it's completely synonymous with so many other things that I'm doing in my life, especially in my work," he says. "Golf is in so many ways a microcosm of life in terms of effective ways to approach it. The beginning of my path back to enjoying golf is to work more on taking credit for the process of approaching it correctly, but then completely surrendering credit or control over the result. If it goes exactly where you needed it to, great; if not, as long as you approached it exactly as you needed to, that's where there's real value. There are a lot of unanswered questions out on the course for me, but more than anything I just feel good when I'm out there and I feel good when I'm done playing a round. I'm growing to love the challenge of it."

James Woods

James Woods is another one of those golfers with beginner's luck. He had been playing the game only a few months when he nearly pulled off a miracle. He was playing the Princeville Golf Club on Kauai when he came to a par 3. "I was lucky to be able to hit the ball then," he says. "I hit a shot that went way to the left out over a big canyon, came all the way back, landed on the green, and rolled right next to the pin. I missed a hole in one literally by an inch. It would have been the most embarrassing hole in one in history, because it went about an extra eighty yards to get there."

That was seven years ago, but it seems Woods plays his best golf in Hawaii. Playing on Lanai recently, he broke 40 on the front side of the difficult Koele course there and wound up shooting an 83, his best ever. "I love the game," says the actor, a 19-handicap and member of Bel-Air Country Club who gets out once a week. "I like being outside, I like the camaraderie, and it's always a challenge."

Robert Wuhl

*O*n his critically acclaimed HBO series *Arli$$*, Robert Wuhl plays a sports agent who's passionate about all sports, but in one episode during the 1997 season he becomes especially obsessed with golf. It's the only sport that will allow him to be "in the arena" with some of the guys he represents when he gets an invite to "the Crosby" (as in Norm, not Bing). Arliss is so intent on playing well that he takes to hitting balls off the balcony of his office. When his back goes out and a pro he represents won't use a wedge he's getting paid big bucks to endorse, it becomes side-splittingly funny. "I had heard stories of pros endorsing products and not using them," Wuhl says. "Anytime I get that kind of thing into the show it's real good. It's something you didn't know."

In real life, Wuhl isn't quite so consumed by the game. A 19-handicap, he plays only about half a dozen times a year. "I can hit a ball a real long way, but I don't have a lot of control," he says. "I hit a lot of balls out-of-bounds. So I'm lucky if I can break 100, but as far as a scramble or a handicap thing, I'm the guy you want."

Such was the case at Raymond Floyd's Lexus Challenge in December of 1996, when he ripped a couple of 300-yard drives and made a hole in one with a pitching wedge from 153 yards. "Joe Pesci was a little pissed off at my handicap. He said, 'Some guys, you've got to really check their handicaps,'" says Wuhl, who got very excited over making his first ace. "Especially because it happened at the

Lexus. But it was the only hole, mind you, that you didn't win a car on. It was sponsored by Alamo Rent-a-Car, so I got an upgrade from subcompact to a midsize on a two-day weekend rental."

Growing up in New Jersey, Wuhl used to caddie at his dad's club, Twin Brooks Country Club in Wachung. One summer when he was about nineteen, he was trying to lose a little weight and went on a restricted diet that limited his salt intake. On one typically hot and humid summer day, Wuhl was struggling under the stress of a double loop and passed out in the middle of the round.

"Here are these four guys in their sixties who are popping nitroglycerin tablets for their hearts," he recalls, "and they have to take this 19-year-old back to the clubhouse in a cart."

He recovered fine after taking some salt tablets and cooling off.

Wuhl used to play a lot as a teenager with his dad, Stanley, a produce distributor. "With my father, you not only had to watch your ball, you had to watch his," he recalls. "He was always saying, 'Where'd it go, where'd it go? Why aren't you watching it, why aren't you watching it?'"

On one particularly soggy day, Stanley took a furious swing from the fairway with a long iron. Mud went flying everywhere. "The ball went straight down, never came up," Robert recalls. "And he's going, 'Where is it, where is it?' I'm dying laughing. I couldn't stop laughing, and he was getting pissed at me. 'Where'd it go?!' I'm just pointing at the ground, because I can't talk. It was the funniest thing I've ever seen."

Index

Maltbie, Roger, 36
Mantegna, Joe, 116–18
Marin, Cheech, 119
Marr, Dave, 62
Martin, Dean, 120–22
Martin, Dick, 123–25
Marx, Harpo, 126–27
Massey, Daniel, 9
Matheson, Tim, 128–30
McClain, Ned, 157
McCord, Gary, 19–22
McGill, Bruce, 129
Meatloaf, 131–32
Menjou, Adolphe, 72
Merrins, Eddie, 23, 40
Mickelson, Phil, 119
Miller, Johnny, 67, 69, 124
Montague, John, 27
Monti, Eric, 126
Moore, Ted, 12
Murphy, Michael, 40
Murray, Bill, 32, 51, 133–38
Murray, Jim, 5, 120–22

N

Nash, Graham, 139–41
Nelson, Byron, 122
Nelson, Craig T., 32
Nichols, Bobby, 123
Nicholson, Jack, 142–44
Nicklaus, Jack, 39, 42, 181,
    182

O

O'Connor, Donald, 145–46
O'Donnell, Chris, 147–51
O'Grady, Mac, 84, 166, 167

Oosterhuis, Peter, 124
Oviatt, Jim, 80

P

Palmer, Arnold, 77, 89, 115,
    149, 192
Pate, Steve, 131
Pavin, Corey, 20, 119
Pesci, Joe, 32, 105, 152–54,
    199
Pickford, Mary, 43
Pohl, Dan, 50
Poitier, Sidney, 81
Poston, Jason, 155–56
Poston, Tom, 155–56
Povich, Maury, 157–59
Povich, Shirley, 157

Q

Quaid, Dennis, 160–61
Quaid, Randy, 160–61
Quayle, Dan, 37

R

Reagan, Ronald, 171
Redford, Robert, 162
Reed, Pamela, 163–64
Regalbutto, Joe, 85, 165–67
Rhoden, Rick, 186
Ribeiro, Alfie, 175
Richards, Ted, 30
Riegert, Peter, 128
Riveria Country Club, 43
Rogers, Ginger, 1
Rogers, Will, 44
Rowan, Dan, 123–24
Rucker, Darius, 152, 168–70